I WAS A HOUSE DETECTIVE

I WAS A
HOUSE DETECTIVE

BY
DEV COLLANS
with
STEWART
STERLING

E. P. DUTTON & CO., INC.

NEW YORK   1954

Library of Congress Catalog Card Number: 54-5047

To all those good friends, the Security Officers with whom I worked, who taught me the angles of the business from sub cellar to roof garden, covered up my blunders, shared with me the credit for their collars, took over on my shift when I couldn't, and by their example helped make me as good a house officer as I was, this volume is dedicated with deep respect for those who are still active and warm regard for the memory of those who have gone.

—DEV COLLANS

CONTENTS

I WAS A HOUSE DETECTIVE

I

Forewarning

LAWS OF LIBEL being what they are—and the peculiar sexual shenanigans which take place in hotel rooms being what *they* are—some of the names in the following pages are fictitious. But none of the facts are. Dev Collans is no creation of a writer's imagination. He's a solid-set, balding, calm-eyed citizen of fifty-nine who wears an eighteen collar and a ten D shoe.

He was born in Toms River, New Jersey, of Irish and English stock. He quit school at thirteen; being big for his age, got a job as bellhop in one of those overgrown Boardwalk boarding houses in Atlantic City—a mustering ground for the rocking-chair brigade of elderly vacationists but also an establishment where conventioneers' week ends might be conveniently lost or casual romances brought to a discreet climax.

After five years of rooming unwed couples and running errands for crochety old ladies he graduated to the post of understudy for the house officer. On that individual's off-days Dev was allowed to swap his monkey suit for a blue serge, quite possibly the youngest hotel detective in the country at that time. A year later he gave up his tips and uniform to become a full-time house officer.

As of today he lives in a six-room house in a Long Island suburb close enough to be reached by subway from New York. Besides the house and a Dodge sedan, he has a wife seven years younger than he is and a son of twenty-six. Mrs. Collans has white hair, a nice smile and (possibly of necessity) a patient disposition. She has a deep freeze and a washing machine; Dev has a lawn mower and a snow shovel, which give him all the summer and winter exercise for which he feels the need after forty years of burning the soles of his feet padding along carpeted corridors.

Because his neighbors like him, because the kids in his block admire him and the women in her church think Mrs. Collans' "scalloped oysters are just about the tastiest thing" at their covered-dish suppers, and particularly because in his retirement the last thing he wants is notoriety, I wholeheartedly agreed when he suggested we conceal his identity under the *nom de hotel* Devlin Collans.

But there were other reasons for not revealing the names of the hotel and the individuals with whose carryings-on Dev was involved during those four decades. Some of the hotels have changed hands; it would hardly be fair to present managements to refer to the lewd and lurid pasts of their establishments. Some of the notorious criminals may have reformed; if so, Dev would want no part in specifying names.

From the writer's standpoint, the major difficulty in getting this inside story of philanderers and prowl teams, of keyworkers and C-girls, of walk-in men and walk-up ladies, was in persuading Dev his recital would serve a useful purpose.

He was troubled lest some readers of this exposé might

be deluded into a false confidence that they, too, might put over a fast one by copying the methods herein described. Not until I'd convinced him that by making it clear to any would-be lawbreaker that the Security Staff in every hotel of size and standing knows all the angles thoroughly, did he agree that the publication of the *modus operandi* might tend to prevent rather than stimulate crime in the vertical cities we call hotels.

Naturally this note of caution isn't addressed to *You*. *You'd* never try to slip an unregistered member of the opposite sex into your room at night or do any of the other evil things described by Mr. Collans. I realize that. Yet there are many who would.

So it is in the genuine hope that the inside information which follows may help *you,* when guest of a hotel, to guard your own property and person, that we reveal the true story of a man who was, for better than a third of a century, one of the best (as well as best-liked) hotel detectives in the business.

STEWART STERLING

II

So I Learned About Women

BELLHOPPING in a big resort hotel was the best possible training for a young man who was going to spend most of his life as a house detective. My five years on the bell captain's staff in Atlantic City taught me about a lot of things. Including women.

I expect that at eighteen I had at least the normal curiosity about sex; there couldn't have been many places better calculated to satisfy that curiosity than a four-hundred-room hotel. On the callow assumption that any girl who would sleep with a man, when not married to him, was immoral, I began to speculate on every couple I roomed.

From other bellboys I learned methods for telling whether a man and woman were a lawfully bedded pair or not. Married couples, for example, never hesitated to open their bags or suitcases while I was still in the room checking on coat hangers, toilet tissues, etc., but unwed parties would never open their luggage while I was in the room.

Clothes told a lot. Honeymooners or newlyweds would generally wear new dresses and new suits and especially new shoes. If the man had expensive clothes, the girl would be fitted out stylishly, too. But if a couple checked in with the man wearing fancy tailor-mades while the girl's shoes, say, were a bit run-down at the heels or her coat showed signs of being three or four years old—I put them down as not legally bonded.

A couple who phoned down for liquor the minute they hit the room were marked as not being legally hitched. Any married woman, on vacation, would have preferred to go out and have a drink, to see something of the town, rather than stay in her room and sip at a highball.

I could generally get some idea of the status by the amount of time a couple spent in their room. Married couples went to bed earlier but the "illegals" stayed in bed longer, mornings.

But what I began to learn about women puzzled me— (not that it hasn't continued to, ever since!) Never did one of those girls whom I fancied as "immoral" give me any occasion to think I might make amorous headway with her. On the other hand, the number of obviously married women who made more or less open advances was astonishing. If it hadn't been for the strict regulations laid down by the Front Office I'd probably have gotten myself in real trouble at least once every week end.

The rules forbade entering the room of a female guest while she was disrobed or in the bathroom, while she was in bed or arising from it. If, by mischance, a bellboy did enter a room where a female guest was partially undressed, he was required to go out to the corridor immediately and, while there, apologize through the closed door.

Many times a woman would answer my knock by calling, "Come in" when she had on nothing except a flimsy bit of lingerie. If I started to back out, she'd make some jesting remark like: "Not afraid of *me,* are you, boy? *I* won't bite you!" or "Haven't you ever seen a girl undressed before? Come on *in.*"

I couldn't begin to list all the dodges a certain type of

woman would try, in order to get a bellboy into bed with them. One common one was to say: "I sat on one of those Boardwalk benches and got some chewing gum on my skirt; do you know how to get chewing gum off?" If you answered that sometimes it could be scraped off with a knife, in nothing flat she'd be taking her skirt off and parading around in her pinkies. . . .

Then there was the "I just *can't* get this thing hooked up!" type, demonstrating how helpless she'd be with corset or brassière—"see if *you* can do it," routine. And the "Ooh, look how *terribly* sunburned I got out on the beach, today!" line, which always necessitated showing the bellboy a lot that wasn't sunburned.

Some of our single women guests were looking for Romance, too . . . and not too fussy about where they found it. Some of these "singles"—stenographers, schoolteachers or salesgirls on vacation—were less artful about what they wanted than the, generally, older married woman: "I've got the funniest *pain* . . . right there . . . come here and rub it for me, like a good boy, will you?" —pointing to some part of her anatomy which I wasn't even supposed to *see*.

I've brought drinks up to the room shared by a pair of sexy "singles" and had one of them ask me in the presence of the other, if I was a virgin . . . or did I know "what it was all about!"

But I had sense enough—or caution enough, perhaps— to realize that while the ladies who liked to show their legs and their lingerie to the bellboy might be numerous, they really were in the minority. And even that minority were probably much more demure at home, for fifty weeks out of the year, than they seemed to be at the beach, during a fortnight's vacation.

Meantime I was learning other things, as well. Especially to size up guests by their appearance, speech, clothing, jewelry, mannerisms and luggage.

It wasn't long before I could make a pretty fair "Guestimate" of the contents of satchels and suitcases while hefting them. A well-packed bag filled with clothing and nightwear has a heft no weighting with books or bricks can duplicate. We had comparatively few overnight guests so we weren't bothered much by the class of patrons who would load a newly bought bag with phone directories to make it look as if they were legitimate travelers. But once in a while I'd grab hold of a satchel which felt as if it might be weighted with a couple of bricks.

This would have suggested I might be rooming a guest who'd eat all his meals at the hotel for five or six days and then depart, wearing beneath his raincoat the few items of clothing he had put in the satchel. The hotel would be left "holding the bag."

I'd make a report of my suspicions to the House Officer, who'd wait until the guest had gone down to dinner, give his room a quick once-over. If there wasn't much clothing hanging in the closet, few items on the bureau and the satchel itself was locked, the house detective would take steps.

Later that night, when the guest was in his room, the House Officer would go up, knock and apologetically announce the Housekeeper had reported a blanket missing. This would be sheer invention; all that would be missing was confidence in the guest's intention to pay. But the H.O. would insist on having the suitcase opened, to make sure no hotel property had been put in it, "by mistake."

If the guest opened the satchel, it would be fairly easy to tell whether the luggage was "loaded" or legitimate; if it was "loaded," the guest would be asked for immediate payment of the bill to date.

In those cases where the guest became indignant and refused to open the suitcase, the House Officer would state he'd have to call in the police, to enforce the law against swindling an innkeeper. The guest would usually pay up and check out immediately.

Some of the other points I picked up were, to mention only a few:

Guests with new or expensive luggage tipped more than those with battered baggage; thus, the man who wanted to create a good impression with his luggage would also want to create a favorable attitude by the size of his tip.

Single men were always better tippers than married men. Single women worse tippers than married women.

Men with fraternal rings or pins in their lapels were always generous. Younger men invariably more so than elderly ones.

Poor tippers were the worst complainers. Part of a bellboy's job was to see that all the electric light bulbs in a guest's room actually worked, that there were clean towels on the rack, that the windows were adjusted to the guest's satisfaction, so on. Busying myself with checking up on such items would, incidentally, give the guest time to fish out a coin for me.

Many times I've had a guest beat me to it, by dashing into the bathroom the instant the door to the room was unlocked. From inside the bathroom would come a muffled: "I'll see you later, bellboy." Never, to my recollection, did one of these "Bathroom Berthas" ever "see me later." But often there'd be a long string of complaints to the linen room; towels were dirty, sheet was torn, no soap in the container, etc., etc.

Bellboys are expected to report to the management such things as firearms in a guest's luggage, or explosives, or large sums in new bills, suggesting the possibility of counterfeit money. It was because of my spotting a revolver in a woman's suitcase that I got my start as an assistant house officer. I couldn't honestly claim much credit for anything except that I kept my eyes open and spotted the gun when she left her suitcase open.

The woman was in her sixties, didn't seem sufficiently well-to-do to require a pistol for protection against robbery. While she was in the dining room our house officer went up, extracted the cartridges from the gun. Later he managed to get into conversation with her. It didn't take long for him to come to the conclusion she planned to kill herself. She was convinced she was suffering from cancer, then considered incurable.

The House Doctor was called in. He was a sympathetic soul, and before long had won the old girl's consent to an examination. It proved that her fears were probably groundless; she had a painful but quite curable stomach ailment.

The House Officer didn't bother to put the cartridges back but he did come around to give me a pat on the back . . . and an offer to act in his place on his off-days.

I jumped at the chance. A bellboy had very little time to himself, he was always "on the stick" to answer the desk bell or busy doing some tiresome errand for a guest who didn't expect to tip anything for it. A House Officer, it seemed to me, was more or less his own boss, free to roam around as and where he saw fit. It was the greener pasture in the field over the fence, and it looked mighty attractive to me.

Not even those first stern instructions made it seem less so:

"First thing you have to remember is to forget everything you've heard about detectives. On this job you won't do any of the things plain-clothes men are supposed to do. No shadowing suspects. No browbeating stool pigeons. No chasing of crooks. A detective has to catch crooks. You're supposed to stop 'em before they do anything crooked."

One of the things I was especially warned about was the method used by the Comeback Kids. That much, at least, I didn't forget.

A Comeback Kid was a room-rifler who operated by the simple procedure of checking in and checking right out again the next day but "forgetting" to turn in the room key when he left. A day or so later he'd come in again, play safe by phoning the room first to make sure the new guest was out. Then the Comeback Kid would simply go up to the room, unlock it as if he still belonged there, rifle the luggage at leisure.

Their favorite time for such operations was during dinner hours from six to eight. Remembering this, every evening, while I was doubling in brass for the regular house officer, I posted myself right close to the two house phones beside the Cashier's desk.

One of those nights a dumpy little man who looked like a grocer came along to use the house phone. He asked the operator to connect him with 563. After a brief pause, he said, "All right," hung up and strolled to the elevator. After a moment's thought, I realized he *couldn't* have spoken to the party in 563 . . . yet he was going right up to the room, knowing the occupant was out!

I sauntered into the elevator after him, being careful not to look at him, yet so self-conscious I was sure he'd sense my nervousness.

At the Fifth he got off. I rode to Six; stepped off after asking the elevator man to send an Assistant Manager to

Five, ran down the stairs in time to see the pudgy party approaching 563 . . . with one of our keys, distinguishable by its triangular wooden tag, in his hand.

I was possibly twenty-five paces behind him when he got the door open. From inside the room I heard a girl cry: *"Oh! What are you doing in my room!"*

The Comeback Kid didn't get rattled a bit. "Didn't realize you were in, Miss," I heard him say. "I'm the House Officer."

She said "Oh!" I could have echoed it, louder.

He went on: "I just rang your room, from downstairs."

I began to wonder if, without my knowing it, somebody'd been put on the job in my place!

She said: "I heard the phone just as I was coming in; I couldn't imagine—"

"We had word," he continued smoothly, "somebody'd smelled smoke up here . . . I just came up to check, that's all."

"Don't you," she asked, "usually knock before you come in a room?"

I'd slowed down a couple of steps from the door, to hear what he had to say.

"We don't after we've called and found the guest isn't in," he answered, backing out practically into my arms.

She said: "If there's any danger of fire, I guess you're going to look in some of the other rooms, too . . ."

That was my cue. "No," I grabbed him from behind, "the only room he's going to look into is a cell over at the police station."

For a little man, he put up a big scrap for a few minutes. He used some alley-gang tactics on me; I was glad when the Assistant Manager came along to help me.

Turned out several other hotels were looking for the

"grocer"—one of them a New York house which presently heard about my part in his capture. The Chief House Officer there wrote me a nice letter stating that if I ever thought of coming to New York there might be a place on his staff for me. Which was how it happened that almost before my Comeback Kid was on his way to prison, I, too, was on my way. In more respects than one.

III

Bags and Baggages

WORKING in a metropolitan house was quite different than parading around the lobby of a resort hotel; there was a lot more for the house officers to do. The first job to which I was assigned, for instance, had nothing whatever to do with guests. It concerned characters inelegantly termed "lobby lice."

These were loungers, loafers and larrikins who hung around annoying, and sometimes swindling, desirable patrons. And these vermin really got in my hair.

Most irritating were the juvenile hoodlums who'd come galloping in from the streets after school was out, making a great disturbance, pestering guests, whooping and hollering.

I'd try to pick out the ringleader and corner him. When I got him, I'd quiz him about his home, parents, school, truancy record—keeping him long enough to make him sweat a bit and perhaps think twice about using our lobby as a public playground again. But next day there'd be another gang boiling in when the doorman was too busy to block them off.

Most numerous of the older lobby lice were the snoozers who'd drop in after lunch to *siesta* in one of our comfortable club chairs. When roused they'd generally crack back at me about "having as much right here as anybody else" . . . which was far from the fact. No one but a registered guest or a patron spending money in bar

22

or dining room is actually entitled to use lobbies, lavatories, and so on. Even this privilege doesn't extend to public napping.

The snoozers had to be moved on for their own protection as well as on account of appearances. A drowsing person was duck soup for pickpockets or bag-grabbers. The napper seldom appreciated this; usually resented being roused.

I found there was a trick to moving them on without unpleasant flare-ups. If I shook the shoulder of a gently snoring man, his reaction often would be a snarled: "What th' hell you think you're doing! Keep your hands off me!" Usually he'd insist he'd only dozed off for a minute, when I'd been watching him for at least five.

Sometimes a woman drowser would claim she'd been "waiting to meet a friend." Or she'd "been meaning to register and stay at the hotel," but of course after I'd awakened her so rudely she'd drive her ducks to another pond!

One waspish female who'd fallen asleep on a bench close to the head of the mezzanine stairs, I'd been worried she might fall off, roll down the stairs, raised a rumpus when I touched her on the shoulder after speaking to her failed to rouse her. She bawled me out in a shrill voice for "making free with her person."

The trick I learned was to beat a sleeper to the punch by firing a question the instant his eyes opened. Such as: "Pardon me, but are you Mister Quilch?"

Generally the napper would answer, "No" before he began his "What the hell you think you're doing!" routine. Before he could get going on that, I'd continue: "Sorry to disturb you, but I'm the house officer. There's a party at the desk inquiring for Mister Quilch. Would you be Mister Quilch?"

23

The drowser would grumble, *"No, I'm NOT!"* but by then he'd be wide awake, would get up and move along, muttering grouchily.

Not all the pests were as harmless as the sleepers; the ones who made the most serious trouble were the Snatchers.

In the course of time I've run into a lot of these parasites. The faces changed from year to year; the methods varied a little as new angles were added but the fundamental principles remained the same. One method, which results in many losses to unsuspecting guests, is the Walkaway.

Say you and your wife arrive at a hotel around six in the evening. The doorman helps you get your luggage out of the taxi. A bellman carries your bags in, sets them on the floor beside the suitcases, hatboxes and overnight bags of a dozen other guests waiting to register.

The lobby is crowded. Clerks are busy checking on reservations, assigning accommodations. Bellmen are rushing in and out of elevators. You line up in the queue at the Room Clerk's desk. Your wife waits close by your luggage, to keep an eye on it.

She pays no particular attention to the prosperous-looking individual who slips into line behind you. But no wife could be expected to ignore a smartly dressed siren who plunges through the throng toward you with hands outstretched as if you were her long-lost darling. Especially when the cutie cries: "Eddie! To *think,* meeting you *here!* Isn't this *won*derful!!"

Now this is calculated to embarrass you; quite likely it does. For one thing, your name (we'll say) *isn't* Eddie. For another, you can't for the life of you recall this excited bit of fluff who seems so delighted to see you again.

24

You don't want to be rude to her; her approach is, to say the least, flattering. But neither do you like the idea that your wife may suspect you of having called yourself Eddie on the occasion of some previous philandering.

For the moment, say thirty seconds, your attention and that of your wife will be pretty well concentrated on the enthusiastic young lady who is, by now, clinging to you, —looking eagerly up into your face, etc., etc. So neither you nor your helpmate are apt to notice the prosperous-looking party who disgustedly pulls out of the line at the desk, calls loudly to a bellman:

"Boy, boy . . . here, take my bags to the checkroom. I can't waste all night checking in. Put those bags—those two there—in the checkroom and bring me the check. I'll wait here." The bags to which he points are yours, but you don't notice that; you're occupied in explaining (a) to the attractive bit of fluff, and immediately thereafter (b) to your wife, that there seems to have been a slight mistake in identity.

But it all seems perfectly legitimate to the bellman. Besides the prosperous-looking party hasn't touched the bags himself; he merely wants them checked.

But the bags don't reach the checkroom. The prosperous party hurries after the bellman, calling, once out of earshot of you and your wife, "Damnit, I forgot! I *can't* check those bags yet! Have to get a couple of things out of them, first. Here—" a fat tip is transferred—"I'll just take them. Thanks."

Before you've even gotten around to the realization you've been robbed, he is Walking Away with your property, out of the hotel, or to some spot where he can ransack the suitcases, remove anything pawnable.

The Walkaway has a hundred variations which all

25

come down to a distraction at the critical time when your luggage has not yet been assigned to the charge of one particular bellman.

Big hotels do the best they can to beat this racket by stationing one of the Security Staff close to the incoming luggage. Often a porter takes a stand by the waiting baggage, too. Bellmen are instructed how the Walkaway scheme works, so they won't fall for it.

Snatchers sometimes go after other things than luggage. Nowadays practically all hotels use brass checks for coatrooms connected with dining rooms, roof gardens, grills, or whatever their nighttime dancing spots are called. But when I started in, many still used numbered cardboard checks. A few still do; many night clubs stick to the printed checks . . . which is why I bring up the matter of Peekers. Though these pests can no longer operate in most hotels, they still get away with expensive coats at certain fashionable hotspots.

Early in the evening, before the tonier customers have begun to arrive in numbers, a couple of Peekers, suitably dressed for admission to one of the zizzier places, waits across the street from the night-club entrance. Presently some limousine or chauffeur-driven convertible rolls up and a couple of socialites disembark. The Peekers quickly cross the street, follow the swank couple in; they have spotted a caracul or a mink or possibly a chinchilla.

At the coat checkroom they crowd close enough to the fur-wearer to peek at the printed number on the check given her escort. The stage is set.

The male Peeker cautiously selects a counterfeit check from a bunch he's had run off by some shady print shop; the duplicate will bear the same number as the one given to the escort of the fur-bearing creature. It will be an excellent imitation of the ones used by the night club. Same weight stock, same color ink, same borders and printing. It will also have been thoroughly handled, spotted and begrimed so as to match the club checks, originals of which were obtained on some previous visit by "losing" a check, taking it away to copy.

The rest is merely a matter of presenting the duplicate check to one of the checkroom girls at a time when the place is jammed with incoming customers. The valuable fur coat goes around the shoulders of the female Peeker; she and her partner stroll out with several thousand dollars worth of furs.

The female Peeker must look like the kind of swanky-pants girl who *might* be wearing that much money on her back. The party from whom the fur is stolen must not be too well-known, otherwise the coat-check girl would remember who the expensive mink belonged to. Consequently the victims are usually out-of-towners.

I once ran into what I figured must be an especially smart pair of Peekers. Eventually I found out they were Quick Changers, operators of a racket which, with some streamlining to bring it up to date, is still worked.

A patron would present his numbered brass check with the hotel's name stamped on it. The attendant would search the shelves for a bag to which had been attached the corresponding duplicate, would come up with some sleazy beat-up piece of luggage a hockshop wouldn't have offered a nickel on. The patron would deny with indignation it was his, would demand his own luggage. But his own cowhide suitcase with all his clothing and valuables, would not be on the shelves.

Since the owner still had his check, the hotel was responsible . . . to the tune of whatever amount the owner felt like claiming . . . within reason. The checkroom attendants were mystified. The Front Office was in a fine lather. And I was on the spot.

My first suspicion was of collusion between an attendant and some snatcher. If the attendant, on receiving an obviously valuable bag to check, had given the patron a tab bearing one number and then fixed the corresponding duplicate to some frowsy old cardboard suitcase, the valuable bag could later have been passed out to a confederate. It would then appear to have been nothing more than a mixup in the checks.

But there were a number of points which weighed against such a suspicion. Both attendants had been with the hotel for years, were highly regarded and trusted absolutely. Also, all these "mistakes" seemed to occur on week ends, generally Friday or Saturday evenings . . . which suggested the professional Snatcher.

After the third such "switch," on a Saturday evening in September when an angry traveling salesman had put in a claim for $600 worth of costume jewelry samples belonging to the Attleboro, Mass., firm which he represented, I made up my mind to get to the bottom of the business if I never cocked another pistol.

The following Friday I camped out in one of the row of phone booths which commanded a sidelong view of the checkroom, about twenty feet distant. Equipped with cigars and an occasional cup of coffee, I watched every patron who brought in a bag or a parcel, every person who took out so much as a topcoat. By midnight, when the checkroom closed, I had nothing but a set of cramped muscles for my pains.

All next day I kept a watch from my two-foot-square sentry box. I was about ready to give up when, along about nine-thirty in the evening, a young fellow bustled past my booth, slapped a check down on the package-room counter. He might have been, in Damon Runyon's words, either a Yale or a Harvard; he looked very collegiate in his smart dinner jacket. But he was really in a sweat; his collar was wilted; his dress shirt was damp.

"Wow!" he panted to the checkroom attendant. "I'm melted down like an ice cream cone at a ball game."

"Been up to the dance?" The attendant referred to some university shindig in the Crystal Room.

"Yeah," the wilted one answered. "I don't want to take my bag out, just want to get a clean collar."

"Seven Oh Two." By prearrangement the attendant read the number off the check loudly enough for me to hear it.

"That's it," the collegian pointed. "That black one with M.S. on the top. Say, all right if I change my collar in there? Only take a sec. I don't want to bother to drag that bag down to the lavatory and back again."

"I guess it's all right." According to hotel regulations, the attendant would have had to check the young fellow's bag out and in again, so the quick-change idea would save trouble all around . . . he thought. He lifted the hinged counter for Collegian to pass through, set the black satchel on the counter running at right angles to the storage shelves.

The wilted one opened his bag, got out a collar, stripped off his coat.

A couple of elderly men brought in brief cases for the attendant to check. No sooner had they gone than a stout man came in with a pelican waddle. He was short and broad with a round, red-tomato face; he planked down a check. "Hot, ain't it?" he panted.

The attendant read out the number on the check. "One Six Five." The suitcase he fetched from the storage shelves was a new one of heavy cowhide, with shiny brass catches.

The One Six Five number didn't ring a bell in my memory but I did recall that new suitcase, for it had a red Cunard sticker pasted on its side. At the time it had come in, around noon, I'd thought as I sized up its owner: "Now you're one gent who *looks* like a man who's just come over First Cabin . . . and maybe a regular seat at the Captain's Table." He'd been tall, thin, pale and kind of haughty, the way some British people impress me; there couldn't have been a greater contrast between him and this Fat Boy who was calling for his luggage.

Fat Boy slapped two-bits on the counter, reached for the cowhide handle. I reached for him.

"Whatsa idea?" His eyes bugged out in astonishment.

"You positive that's your suitcase?" I asked.

Just then the Collegian, still fingering his fresh collar, swung up the hinged section of the counter, came through to my side. I fingered his collar, too . . . not as tenderly as he'd been touching it.

Fat Boy turned to squirm away. Collegian took a poke at me. The attendant grabbed him. We wrestled them around to a service elevator, up to my office.

Then I asked the attendant if there'd been quite a bit of that collar-changing business recently. He admitted there had been. He hadn't seen any harm in it; he'd been right there all the time so the Quick-Changers couldn't have taken anything out of any luggage except their own.

I told him maybe Collegian couldn't have opened any other bags but while the attendant's back had been turned, as in the instance of the two old gentlemen with the brief cases, Collegian could easily have switched duplicate checks on two bags. It would only have taken a second to exchange the duplicate on One Six Five, which turned out to be a broken-down Gladstone not worth half a buck, to the handle of some valuable piece like the cowhide suitcase.

Then Fat Boy, who'd originally checked the worthless Gladstone, could have rushed in and hustled out with the luggage of the distinguished-looking Britisher. That is, he'd have hustled out with it if we hadn't hustled him off to the police station.

In one of the Marx Brothers pictures there was a bit of dialogue between a *grande dame* who wanted information about getting a room in the seaside resort run by Groucho, I believe. She inquired what they had overlooking the front of the house. Groucho replied by introducing her to Chico who was playing the part of a house detective.

But I was learning that no house officer could overlook much and keep his job—off the screen.

IV

Have You a Woman in Your Room?

WHEN I started out as a house officer I had great hopes of developing what I'd heard called "the camera eye," the ability to remember a countless number of faces and to recognize them after a long interval. It didn't take me more than a couple of months to discover that ability of that sort simply doesn't exist. Even if it did, it wouldn't be very useful.

In some of the hotels, at which I've been employed over a forty-year period, as many as ten thousand people would move in and out of the lobbies every day. No human being can make mental notations about the characteristics of more than three and a half million people every year.

Those desk clerks who "never forget a face," the "greeters" who recall the guest's name though he hasn't stopped at the hotel in years, have trained their memories to a fine point by concentrating on a certain class of transients. Usually business executives; one-third of all the people in the average hotel will be businessmen between the ages of thirty and fifty.

Plain-clothes men who can spot a pickpocket in a crowd, years after first seeing him in a police lineup, work in the same way. They concentrate on a comparatively small group.

I learned to do this, to a degree—where hotel crooks were concerned—though I never got to the point of really being cocksure of the identities of certain customers I thought I recognized as room-riflers, skippers, etc. Too many folks resemble other folks closely enough to make it risky to walk up to a man, tap him on the shoulder and say: "Come along quietly."

The answer was to pay more attention to peoples' mannerisms than to their ear lobes or jawbones. The way they walked, moved, gestured; their attitudes at the desk, around the lobby, in elevators, at bars.

A man may grow a beard and wear dark glasses to alter his appearance, but if he still strides through the lobby with a deck hand's rolling swagger, fingers his left lapel while he's waiting for the clerk to see whether there's a nice double available and tilts his head over toward his right shoulder when he signs the registration card, chances are I'll recognize him if I've ever seen him before.

A lady of the evening may dye her hair, switch her

style of clothes and wear low heels instead of high. If she doesn't change the peculiar slouchy stance in which she waits for her pick-up to register or hasn't gotten over that little habit of inspecting her fingernails and absently buffing them on the sleeve of her coat, likely enough I'll remember her.

The real importance of observing mannerisms comes in connection with people who aren't criminals at all, but who may, nevertheless, be trying to put one over on the hotel. Generally they're trying to save a little money by getting more than they expect to pay for. Naturally most of these cases concern women, though not all. There are, for instance, the Camp-Outs.

A Camp-Out is generally a youngster in town during a holiday recess from college or maybe just taking a look at the Big Town during summer vacation. I'd see a couple of obvious undergrads check in for a double around six o'clock; generally they'd want the lowest priced room they could get. Their luggage would be good, and there'd be a lot of it. Usually a couple of suitcases apiece, perhaps a brief case or two in addition.

Too much baggage for a couple of lads who'd answered the room clerk's query about length of stay with "just for tonight and tomorrow." I'd have a pretty good idea right then what was going to happen.

They wouldn't spend much time in their room during the evening . . . or much money, either. Usually there'd be no room-service charges, sometimes a few phone calls. They'd go out for supper.

Around midnight or a little after they'd return. They'd have had a few beers or enough drinks to make them feel like men-about-town. With them would be a couple of other lads about the same age, occasionally three or four others.

33

They'd be nicely mannered and quiet as you please in lobby and elevators. But around 2 A.M. likely I'd get a complaint from one of the adjoining rooms: "Say! There's a terrible racket in the next room! I can't sleep! Can't you get 'em to keep quiet?"

Now sometimes it's a delicate matter to crash in on a party, ask them to tone it down. One of the group making hey-hey may get ugly or try to show off by busting the house officer in the nose. You have to handle liquored-up people with kid gloves. But these Camp-Outs were a different proposition.

When I'd go up with one of the assistant managers, I knew before the door was opened what we'd find. In the room, roughhousing and horsing around in pajamas or shorts would be four or five or six hilarious and slightly tight youths.

There'd be rolled-up coats on the carpets for pillows, overcoats or raincoats as sheets, blankets and maybe the spread from the bed arranged on the floor. And on chairs, dresser and against the walls would be all four suitcases . . . open. A quick glance at the contents would show separate shaving kits or toothpaste in each one. All four (or five or six) were Camping Out for the price of a double.

I seldom had much difficulty with kids like that. Sometimes when I asked the campers to break it up, get dressed and leave they simply had the Assistant Manager call the desk and assign them another room, or two, if it was needed. Once in a while, if they admitted they were short on funds, we'd compromise and let six stay in two doubles.

But Camp-Outs were the least of my troubles. The real problems were the female of the species, the Legits and the Illegits.

34

There was, for instance, the nasty-tempered Legit in 712; I had reason to remember her. I saw her first around one o'clock in the mornnig—a chill, snowy morning in January. She came into the lobby alone, very smartly dressed, not especially good-looking but fresh and whole-some with cheeks rosy from the cold, and a sparkle in her eyes. She marched straight toward the central bank of elevators as if she'd used them often before.

I couldn't place her, but that didn't mean much because we staggered our tours of duty in the Security Office and I'd come on at eight o'clock. But two things about her caught my eye. She had only a small evening bag with her, a tiny item in gold brocade. She didn't open it, on her way to the elevator, as nine out of ten women guests would, to make sure they had their room keys. And she didn't go near the desk to ask if there'd been any mail or phone calls for her.

A well-gotten-up woman like that will generally, if she is in the hotel alone, be anxious about messages. So I guessed she wasn't soloing. But if she'd been out that late, why hadn't her husband been with her? I thought perhaps he had been.

When the elevator came down to the lobby again I glanced across at the operator, cupping my hand behind my ear as if to listen to someone at a distance. He stuck up two white-gloved fingers of one hand and held the other hand up with all fingers and thumb extended.

At the desk I asked the rack clerk to let me know if there'd been any P.I.A.'s on the seventh. He said a Mister P——, from Larchmont, N.Y., had checked in 712 at 12:45 A.M. with no luggage . . . and had Paid in Advance.

Most people have the idea—particularly if they've been used to stopping at motels when touring cross-country—

that paying for a room in advance insures their being considered respectable. Quite the contrary, as will follow . . .

I picked up the house phone, asked the switchboard operator to check with the other girl then on duty to see if any call had come in within the past half-hour for a Mister P——, without the caller specifying the room number. Happened she'd taken the call herself ten minutes before. It had been from a pay station; she'd heard the coin bell. The caller'd been a woman.

I was reasonably sure I knew what had happened. Mr. and Mrs. P—— had come to the city, from the suburban town in which they lived, to have a night out on the town. Probably they'd gone to a musical, had a late supper at one of the chi-chi spots afterward . . . and missed the last train home. They'd decided to stay in town overnight.

But by this time, I figured they'd have spent more money than they'd intended. The idea of forking over eight or nine dollars for a double when they might get away with paying only for a single had occurred to them, just as if they'd been the first couple in the world to scheme up such a smart idea.

So Mr. P—— had probably come in by himself, registered as a single, gone upstairs, having paid in advance because he had no luggage . . . though any good hotel will take the word of a well-dressed guest of substantial appearance as to meeting his bill on the morrow . . . *providing he's alone*. Mr. P—— had given himself away, as so many do, by a guilty conscience . . . knowing he wasn't *going* to spend the night alone.

A little while after he'd registered, Mrs. P—— had called up, from the drugstore at the corner of the avenue a block away, I guessed, and he'd told her what room he had.

36

When I knocked at the door of 712, Mr. P—— seemed startled, asked me to wait a minute. On his opening the door there was no visible evidence of Mrs. P——, but the bathroom door was closed . . . not an ordinary thing in a room occupied by a man alone.

I explained apologetically that females were forbidden in the rooms of male guests. He'd gotten over his surprise by then; didn't make any attempt to deny she was there. But he said the lady was his wife, she certainly had a perfect right to be there. She'd been in town, had missed her train, knew he'd be staying at our hotel, had unexpectedly come on up to stay with him. Nothing wrong with that, was there?

The Assistant Manager who was with me explained the only thing wrong was the little matter of four dollars additional when the room was occupied by two. Ordinarily a Legit's husband would have reached for his wallet, the Assistant Manager would have produced a joiner for signature . . . and that would have been the end of it. But finding their plan for saving a few bucks, at the hotel's expense, frustrated, Mrs. P—— rushed out of the bathroom spitting fire.

She resented our insinuations that her husband had been intending to cheat the hotel. He'd been planning to pay her additional share when they checked out in the morning. *She* knew what we *really* meant by breaking in on them like this! If we thought we were going to get away with humiliating *her,* by treating them as if they *weren't* married, she'd have plenty to say about *that!*

She did. Though Mr. P—— tried to calm her, she went into a regular tirade about suing the hotel for some astronomical figure.

It took a few minutes to set her straight. At no time, I explained carefully, had there been any suggestion she wasn't Mr. P——'s lawful wedded wife. The Assistant Manager was witness to that. Moreover, if she was under the illusion that people could collect damages from hotels because of fancied insults about their marital status, she was 100 per cent wrong.

Probably she'd heard some of those fancy fables about the couple—Mrs. So-and-so had it straight from her cousin who knows them well—who settled out of court for $50,000 or $25,000 (the figures are always attractively high) because some dumb house detective made the mistake of suggesting that a woman who looked like a two-buck tramp wasn't really the legal spouse of her bedmate, when she had been. Those yarns are just so much parsley.

Years ago there were a few instances of this sort of holdup, since then courts have recognized it as a racket. Legal precedents have been established, giving hotels the right to investigate guests in any way, if there is the slightest suspicion of fraud or a question as to the guest's desirability *as* a guest. But it took a while to convince Mrs. P——.

Even then she didn't give up. She was one of those Legits, and I've run into a lot of them, who Have Important Connections. I forget whether she knew our Resident Manager's uncle or the sister-in-law of our Board Chairman. But I'd hear more about it.

It goes without saying, I never did.

For every Camp-Out or Legit who tried to put one over, however, we had to deal with a dozen Illegits. An Illegit is not always a streetwalker or a call girl; she may not be, in the strict sense of the word, a prostitute at all.

In cases where the Illegit *is* a prostitute, it's usually easy to recognize her unless she comes in during the dinner rush or the after-theater jam when we may be too

38

busy to spot her. If she isn't what the boys on the beat call "a regular," often she will still give herself away by her actions and mannerisms.

First of all, an Illegit invariably seems to be in a hurry. Maybe this is because she thinks an appearance of being in haste makes her seem more like a respectable guest anxious to return to her room. Possibly she figures the less time spent where a house officer might observe her, the better. If she realized that a girl, by herself, striding nervously toward the elevators is more conspicuous than one who casts an occasional leisurely glance around . . . especially at other women . . . she might change her tactics. Somehow the pattern never changes.

Like the Legits, the Illegits ignore the desk, walk straight to the elevators. They don't, of course, leave a Morning Call at the desk. None of them ever has foresight enough to show a key in the car going up, something almost all people do.

Elevator men often catch onto the Illegits because of their failure to say "Good night" when let off at their floor. Since most of them come in at a late hour and clearly intend to remain overnight, this is very noticeable. Four out of five women, returning to their room when alone will call " 'Night" to the Up-car operator on quitting the elevator at a late hour.

Room-service waiters or the bellmen are our chief source of tip-offs on such ladies of leisure.

The case of poor Henry White will illustrate. He won't mind my using the name by which he registered; it wasn't his real one. He was a tall, unhappy-looking, string bean of a man in his mid-thirties, pale and washed out. He was a sales clerk in a retail shoe store in Delaware. He'd come to New York for the first time in his life on a forty-eight hour bus excursion and a shoestring budget. Naturally

39

he wanted to have a high time and to stretch that shoe-string as far as it would go.

He had Room 402, one of the worst rooms in the hotel and the lowest priced. It was next to an elevator and on a low floor. Room-service calls from that room were not customarily frequent or for large amounts. On the one night Henry spent at the hotel, he called for room-service only once. About quarter to twelve he phoned down for one rye highball and a *creme de menthe frappé*.

In my book, not many men go for *creme de menthe frappé* at midnight. And when our bellman delivered the liquor, there was only Henry to be seen in the room. While the shoe salesman was assembling silver enough to tip the bellman, the latter was using his eyes.

The bathroom door was open but the closet door was closed. Henry was smoking a pipe but a cigarette fumed on the bureau ash tray. These suggestive points were, in due time, brought to my attention.

I informed the night Assistant Manager that one of our guests seemed to be putting on a romp in 402.

After giving Henry time to get started on whatever he had a mind to, we went up, listened at the door. We heard a woman's voice.

At that moment, according to tradition, I should have made the famous inquiry which has for years been accepted as the house detective's badge of office: "Do you have a woman in your room?" Only it isn't done that way any more.

The Assistant Manager went down the hall, used the floor phone. "Are you," he inquired politely of Henry, "entertaining a lady?"

Henry was shocked . . . almost into incoherence. Finally, and perhaps after some *sotto voce* prompting from

40

the Illegit, he admitted there *was* a lady in his room. His wife. She'd just happened to drop in, unexpectedly.

Not having seen the lady, we weren't prepared to question his word. It's policy, in cases where there has been no unseemly disturbance, to give the guest the benefit of all possible doubts.

So the Assistant Manager came back. I insisted Henry open up. After a brief delay, he did.

The lady was invisible behind the closed bathroom door.

We presented the joiner . . . usual form for signature . . . and a request for three additional dollars.

Henry was embarrassed. He—well—the plain truth was he didn't happen to *have* three additional dollars, at the moment. If it would be all right to wait until morning, though . . .

"Now," I said.

Henry got red in the face. He stammered. He gave us his faithful promise to come through first thing in the morning, before breakfast even . . .

"Right now," I insisted.

He went pale as one of the rumpled pillow slips on the bed. He sidled over to the bathroom door, put his face close to it.

"Honey," he called hoarsely, "could you let me have three dollars back until morning?"

We had to make that a "put-out" for the girl. But I didn't have the heart to put Henry out. He wouldn't have been able to pay for a room anywhere else.

The dame had taken every last cent of his cash.

41

V

Corridor Creeps

FROM the guest's standpoint, the most important employee in a hotel is the Assistant Manager. If the room you've been given has only a tub when you requested a shower, the Assistant Manager is the man to see that you get switched to the proper scrubbing accommodations. If those pals you invited up for a few nightcaps insist on barber-shopping *Down By The Old Mill Stream* at 1 A.M., the next voice you will hear will be that of an assistant Manager, requesting quiet.

The boys with the *boutonnieres* are the hotel's trouble shooters. As such, they work closely with the Security Staff, and *vice versa*. If one of the Assistant Managers . . . (generally there'll be two or three on duty at the same time in a large metropolitan hotel) . . . gets wind of any rough stuff, first thing he does is to notify the Security Chief. If a house officer discovers he has to deal with a difficult guest or a suspected crook, before he takes any drastic action he gets hold of the Assistant Manager so the hotel may have competent witnesses in case of a possible lawsuit.

An Assistant Manager with calm nerves and good judgment can be a big help to the Security men who work with him. One who gets rattled in an emergency or is a bad judge of human nature can be a perpetual pain to his house officers. Stanley A——, who was with the Boston hotel where I held the post of Chief for several years, was a distinct boon to the aspirin business.

Stanley looked the part of an Assistant Manager. He was a dapper dan of about thirty, slim, a little below medium height, quick and nervous in his movements, which gave him a curious air of being simultaneously vain and suspicious. He was, too.

Stanley became very unpopular with our bell captains and desk clerks. Maybe he thought that he had to trample on the feelings of inferiors to climb that old ladder, or possibly he was simply a stickler for regulations. In any case, our lobby crew put him down as a stinker.

He was forever nosing around the bell captain's desk to check on the Time Started and Time Finished entries made in the Bell Ledger. Bellmen weren't supposed to leave the hotel while on duty or in uniform. But often some guest would want a purchase made at one of the stores a couple of blocks away—I remember one boy who made three trips to get the right kind of girdle for an old girl.

If it wasn't rush hour for check-ins or the busy departure-hour in the afternoon, usually a bellman would be glad to oblige the guest who needed a pair of specs taken to the optometrist or a new Cuban heel on a pair of ladies shoes. These courtesy errands built good will. Also, they generally produced juicy tips, and these, by custom, the bellman split with his captain.

Stanley developed an uncanny ability to sniff out any bellman who was absent overlong from the lobby. What was worse, he insisted on reporting these infractions to the Front Office Manager. After he'd made trouble for practically every boy on the day side, they began to lay for him. He was an easy target.

For example, one duty of an Assistant Manager is to

43

watch out for objectionable characters lounging around the lobby. A bellman would confide to Stanley that a character up on the mezzanine was making annoying remarks to ladies. Somehow the information would be passed along when there was no house officer around to make an investigation. So Stanley would take it on himself. Of course when he'd dashed up to the mezzanine there'd be no one there but a mild-mannered minister or perhaps a shy, small boy.

Another duty assigned to Assistant Managers is helping to register guests at peak check-in periods, particularly to take care of prominent individuals who may want to check in as Not Registered, so their room phone won't be rung every fifteen minutes by some newspaper reporter or busybody.

Scarcely a rush hour would pass without some page boy or bellman mumbling indistinctly to Stanley about "the Senator" (or "the Ambassador's wife" or "the Rear Admiral") over there, with no one paying any attention to him. Stanley would always bite and scurry around buttonholing machinery salesmen or deaf old ladies under the misapprehension they were persons demanding his special attention.

Stanley was such an eager-beaver he was continually being victimized by his own stupid judgment. One time the suggestion was made to him that a young lady, hanging around the main desk and obviously ill-at-ease, might be a Key Picker. He sauntered stealthily toward her, watched her out of the corner of his eye for a few minutes, and jumped to a reckless conclusion.

He knew all about Key Pickers; he'd learned the hotel business through the process known as "coming up through the front of the house." This involves working at a succession of jobs dealing directly with guests. Before being promoted to an Assistant Managership, Stanley'd been an Information Clerk, a Transportation Clerk, a Key Clerk, an Assistant Room Clerk and finally, a Chief Room Clerk.

All these jobs come under the supervision of the Front Office Manager, who is also boss over several hundred other employees: the doorman who helps you out of the taxi, the bellman who lugs your suitcase, the clerk who assigns your room, the credit manager who okays your check, the cashier who receipts your bill, many others. Bookkeepers, typists, phone girls, accountants, office boys, secretaries, file clerks, and so on.

It isn't considered necessary for the candidate for an Assistant Managership to have actual experience at all of these occupations. But he *is* supposed to gain knowledge of guest problems by working a few months in most of the jobs behind the desk.

While Stanley'd been Key Clerk it had been rumored a Picker had been working the house. We never caught him or her, but Stanley hadn't forgotten how they operated. A Key Picker loiters near the desk until some guest, on leaving the hotel, drops his key on the counter in front of the key clerk and hurries away. While the clerk has his back turned or his attention distracted, the Picker simply reaches out for the key, goes upstairs, loots the room at leisure. A brazen technique of this sort is especially effective at rush hours.

It was during the noon rush, about half-past twelve, one Saturday in November, when Stanley was tipped off to this ill-at-ease young lady. Guests coming down from their rooms, after freshening up for lunch, were crowding up to the desk, tossing keys on the counter, milling

45

around. Suddenly Stanley saw the young lady reach out a gloved hand, draw it back with a key in it, head hastily for the elevators.

Stanley caught up with her as she was about to step into an Up car:

"One moment, please." He drew her aside. "Are you registered, here at the hotel?"

"N . . . n . . . no!" she stammered in confusion.

"This way, please." He pushed her toward the mezzanine stairs; the Security Office in that hotel was on the mezz.

Up to that point he hadn't handled the matter too offensively, even if he'd used bad judgment in putting the arm on her without being *sure* she'd done something wrong. But having leaped that far toward his dumb conclusion, he then had to get way in over his head by refusing to listen to her excited attempts at explanation.

By the time he'd hustled her into my office she was in a rage . . . and almost hysterical.

How, Stanley protested to me a few minutes later, could he have been expected to know the girl hadn't snitched a key from the desk at all? That she'd merely started to turn in a key which she'd been holding right along, a key to which she'd had a perfect right, and then had abruptly changed her mind?

Why, he demanded dismally, hadn't she instantly told him she'd had, in her purse, one of those little Permit slips issued by the Desk and signed by her aunt, who *was* a guest? The girl made it angrily clear; Stanley hadn't given her any chance to explain that she'd been waiting for her aunt, had finally given up, decided to go upstairs by herself.

Stanley was too busy making excuses to remark on the stroke of bad luck which had made him select as a victim for false accusation a young lady whose name on the Key Permit would immediately have warned him she might be related to the hotel's principal legal counsel! How could he possibly have guessed his supposed Picker was the niece of one of Boston's most prominent attorneys!

The steam was really bubbling in the young lady's gauges at what she called "a most disagreeable man-handling," when she happened to mention that after the game she'd talk to her uncle, who'd *do* something about the distressing rudeness she'd had to put up with. Remembering that the local football shindig of the afternoon was the Harvard-Dartmouth game, I asked if she was sitting on the Green side or the Red?

Turned out she had a brother on the Hanover team, a second-string end. Auntie had come clear up from Indiana to see him play.

I was a Dartmouth rooter myself. Being members of the same Admiration Society made it easier for me to get away with a suggestion that the little misunderstanding down in the lobby didn't really call for penalizing anyone. So Stanley didn't lose his job that time.

He seemed to be mildly grateful . . . but he wasn't chastened a bit. It was only a couple of months later that he pulled another offside play, one which had more serious consequences.

It had to do with the most dangerous sort of crook who works in hotels, a Corridor Creep. This is an ugly customer who may combine any or all of the traits of sneak thief, burglar and gozzler.* He operates late at night, or more accurately, in the early hours of the morning, getting into guests' rooms while they are asleep. As is the case with some second-story workers, the Creep

---

* *A throttler, one who gozzles his victim by choking, sometimes to death.*

47

only becomes genuinely dangerous if and when discovered. He may then kill to prevent an alarm being raised.

This is extremely infrequent, for reasons which will appear; in modern hotels it won't *ever* happen if the guest is careful about elementary precautions. But the danger does sometimes exist, and in hotels not equipped with modern locks (also, in many motels because of the ground-floor situation) it *can* happen any night.

Up until the introduction of the modern pin-tumbler lock (Yale, Segal and similar types) the Creep used to employ skeleton keys. Working from 3 to 5 A.M., when most guests sleep heavily, the procedure was to fiddle with the skeleton key until a lock turned. Then the Creep would quietly open the door a few inches, wait . . . and listen.

If the guest's regular breathing indicated he or she was asleep, and not shamming, the crook would drop down on hands and knees, creep in, swiftly go through the guest's clothes for cash. This type of prowler seldom bothered with jewelry or other valuables.

Often Creeps would check into the hotel, in order to have a plausible explanation if challenged by a corridor patrol.

In the days when even the better class of hotels depended on the old-fashioned "kitchen-door" type of lock, sometimes the Creep used a cute little tool called the *outsiti*. This was a thin-nosed tweezer-type pair of pliers with tiny, concave lips. It was small enough to be shoved into a keyhole; the miniature lips could clamp around the end of a key. With the *outsiti*, the Creep could open a door even when the key'd been left in the lock in accordance with the hotel's official warning.

Nowadays, the Creep has to depend more on human frailty than on mechanical contrivances. Either he lurks in a corridor waiting for some guest who has returned from a bout with Ned Ninety-Proof or he locates his drunk-dazed victim in a bar or café and trails him, or her, to the hotel. People who've had "one over the eight," as the bartenders say, often neglect to lock their doors.

Such a guest is easy prey. Outside in the corridor, the Creep waits until the light in the room has been put out and until he's convinced, from the absence of any sounds other than snores, that the intoxicated guest is temporarily dead to the world. With the door unlocked, the procedure is the same as just mentioned. Open a crack, pause, listen. Then, in a couple of minutes, the Creep is in and out again, with whatever cash the sleeper had in wallet, purse or pants.

Sometimes the sleeper wakes up. Or is only playing possum. Then there's the chance of violence with fatal results, *if* the Creep is sufficiently afraid of an outcry to try and silence the guest. House officers have an understandably deep-rooted dislike for middle-of-the-night marauders, which will explain my actions on that January night in Boston.

I was asleep in the Security Suite when the phone began to do nipups on my bed table. My wristwatch said quarter to four when I switched on the light, grabbed the receiver.

"Mister Collans . . . ? Mister A—— wants you at Eight Seventeen right away . . . Eight Seventeen . . . !"

"What is it? A fight?" I asked.

"I *guess* so," the operator cried. "Some woman up there started to holler into the phone. Then I heard a man yelling at her that she couldn't get away with it, she couldn't put over anything as raw as that . . . and she screeched for the police. So I notified Mister A—— right away. He's gone up."

49

"Okay." I had my pants on by then. "I'm on my way." Within half a minute, I was.

The elevator was at the mezz, waiting for me. The boy on the car exclaimed:

"Somebody goin' t' get hurt up there, Mister Collans . . . way they're carryin' on."

When I stepped off at the eighth floor, it certainly sounded like it. A man and a woman were hollering at each other at the top of their lungs . . .

"You nasty rotten little sneak!" The woman.

"You goddam tramp! Gettin' me up here, then puttin' the B on me! Twenty bucks! You couldn't get twenty cents out of me!!" The man.

And Stanley, shrill. *"Cut it out, now. Both of you! Stop this shouting! You . . . ! Get your clothes on!"* My Assistant Manager trembled with rage, there in the doorway of 817.

I peeked over his shoulder. In the bed was a good-looking blonde in her thirties, the Navy would have described her as "well-stacked." She had on a blue night-gown as transparent as the cellophane on a pack of cigarettes. She was thoroughly mad . . . and, I thought, very scared. She didn't pay the least attention to Stanley, just screamed insults at the man by the bureau.

He was a little older than she was—a well-fed, well-set-up fellow with a butcher's florid complexion and a bristly black moustache. He was slightly bald and half naked. His coat and trousers had been tossed over the back of a chair and his shorts were on the floor. He still had his shirt on, though his necktie'd been loosened as if he'd been about to take it off.

He was paying a little more attention to Stanley and to me than the woman was; he seemed resentful, maybe embarrassed, but not scared.

50

Stanley whispered behind his hand: "She's plastered to the ceiling; I saw her come in half an hour ago; she could hardly hit the floor with her feet."

The woman howled: ". . . *try to pretend I asked you to come to my room, you filthy thief! . . . I never laid eyes on you until I snapped on the light!"*

The man snarled: *"All right! . . . ALL right!! So you thought you could frame me for a sucker! These hotel guys in on it, too?"*

That struck me as a wrong note. If the fellow *had* been lured to the woman's room by a promise of intimacies, only to find out she'd wanted money for her favors, he wouldn't have wanted to antagonize us. At least not until he'd found out whether we'd be on his side, or hers. He'd want to get out quietly, with no possibility of publicity.

But Stanley said, over his shoulder: "Get him out quick's you can, Dev. I'll get the doc down here if she keeps up this racket, give her a shot to keep her quiet."

The blonde kept on screeching. According to her, the fellow'd been completely dressed when she'd surprised him at her purse, by switching on the light at her bed table. He'd only whipped off his pants when she'd grabbed up the phone, hollered for help. Now according to her, he was pretending she'd asked him to come up to her room when actually he was just a sneak thief. The clothes-off business was to give him an alibi.

The man kept on dressing while he appealed to us. He'd made a mistake all right, but it was the sort of thing that might happen to anyone who met a tricky bitch like that blonde. We could ask her if she hadn't given him the old come-on over at L——'s bar, on School Street. We could even ask the bartender who'd served her about six Scotches the embarrassed gentleman had paid for.

Stanley was convinced the blonde was a Commercial

Artist . . . and acted toward her as if he thought so.

I had the feeling the fellow's line was too pat. Possibly he'd seen the girl in L——'s, had trailed her to the hotel, come up in the elevator with her and hung around in the corridor until he'd made sure she'd neglected to lock her door. The rest would have been regular Creep routine.

When he had his clothes on, I took him to the elevator, leaving Stanley sternly reprimanding the blonde, by that time incoherent with fury.

In the elevator I backed the butcher-faced gent in a corner, frisked him. He got pretty sore about it; I had to rough him up a bit before I could go through his pockets. He didn't have any weapon on him. But in his inside coat pocket I found four folded pieces of Bristol board, light cardboard.

They were the printed diagrams of the floor plans of four hotels on Washington, Boylston and Tremont Streets. The sort you find posted in every corridor and sometimes in every room so guests may be able to find their way to the exits, in case of fire.

That was enough for me. I rang the precinct, turned him over to the police . . . with what seemed to me conclusive evidence he'd been primed for room-rifling. The police court magistrate thought I was right about it, too; he was held for the Grand Jury, indicted for attempted robbery . . . with indecent exposure thrown in as an additional charge, for good measure.

Unfortunately there wasn't any conviction. The blonde refused to appear in court against him. Her resentment boomeranged against the hotel management, on account of Stanley's attitude toward her. There was quite a to-do in the Front Office, and Stanley looked for another connection.

52

I've always thought the blonde was lucky, challenging a Creep and not getting choked or at least belted over the head for her courage. The Creep wasn't quite so lucky because they held him in jail long enough to discover he had some "short time" against him on a previous sentence from which he'd been paroled. So he went back to Danvers to serve out his term . . . and probably, to think up some new scheme for robbing hotel guests.

Stanley couldn't seem to get another job in any of the Boston houses, so he drifted down south. Last I heard of him he was working in a second-rate commercial house in Atlanta. He was still an Ass. Manager.

VI

Never Welcome After Twelve

AFTER COMING into the hotel business through the back door, so to speak, in Atlantic City, I was scarcely inclined to take people at face value. It did come natural to me, though, to think the best I could of everyone, until I had good reason to believe otherwise. It sort of went against my grain when I found out that house officers have to get in the habit of thinking the worst of people. It took quite a while for me to realize that a constantly suspicious attitude was an absolute necessity in my line of work.

It was easy to be skeptical about men. Within a year after coming to work for the Chief House Officer (nobody called us Security Men, those days) in a midtown

New York hotel, I'd caught onto many of the giveaway mannerisms which would tip me off to a man who thought he was getting away with something.

Take a man I had occasion to remember as Maurice Wood. A successful young business executive, he had a wife and two youngsters living in a fashionable New Jersey suburb. He also had a smart, attractive . . . and willing . . . secretary working for him in his office.

One evening he phoned his wife that he'd be working late, would stay in town to avoid the long trip out to Jersey and back. Around ten, after he and his amiable assistant had dined and had a few drinks, they agreed the work could just as conveniently be continued in the privacy of a hotel room.

So he phoned our hotel for a reservation, "a twin-bed double high up on the quiet side." They took a taxi back to his office where he got the suitcase which was carefully stored away for such clandestine stopovers. Then they went out and shopped at one of the open-till-midnight Broadway lingerie shops, getting a fancy pair of pajamas for the young lady. From the store they taxied to the hotel.

The doorman helped them out of the cab. The bellman took the suitcase, though the girl held onto the parcel with the pajamas. In the lobby she dropped into one of the overstuffed chairs while her "husband" went to the desk. He signed the registration card as Mr. and Mrs. Maurice Wood, Pittsburgh, Pa., no street address. After being assigned a room, he returned to the girl, nodding to her and saying "All set, hon," or words to that effect.

They followed the bellman to the elevator completely confident that they had been accepted as a properly respectable married couple. They certainly would have been shocked if they'd known that even at that early stage of the game I'd given the bellman the high sign to "put the latch on." They were on my observation list for half a dozen different reasons.

In the first place, if the man and his wife had just arrived in town, *via* train or bus, ordinarily only ten or fifteen minutes would have elapsed between the time of telephoning his reservation and his arrival at the hotel . . . whereas it had been almost an hour. (The time had been stamped on the reservation memo as it was, also, recorded on the check-in card.) People who've been traveling for some hours almost invariably want to get to a hotel room as soon as possible, to wash up and get out of travel-soiled clothing; even if they have some shopping to do it is usually delayed until after they've been settled in their room.

In the second place, a well-dressed couple, as these people were, wouldn't travel any distance with just one suitcase. Certainly not from western Pennsylvania. A married woman would have had some luggage of her own, even if it was only an overnight bag or a hatbox.

Third, the paper parcel, wrapped in the swanky gray-blue-and-silver paper of a well-known Broadway specialty shop, told its own story as plainly as if it had been a placard. "I have a new nightgown," it said, "or some briefies . . . or pajamas."

There were other suggestive points. Mr. "Wood" hadn't put down a street address, possibly because he wasn't sure of a proper residential street in Pittsburgh to *put* down. He hadn't asked any questions, such as: "Can I get my suit pressed this late?" or "Do you have over-night laundry service?"

Then, he hadn't done what most *young* men would

55

have, mentioned the room rate to his wife. Besides, no young wife would have appeared uninterested in how much they were being charged.

Finally, there was the way he half-put his arm around her as she rose from the overstuffed chair, the way he took her elbow as they crossed to the elevator. Unless the man is in uniform, indicating that he may be having a reunion with his wife after a long absence, you don't often see married couples acting that affectionately in public. Always excepting honeymooners, to be sure.

The "Woods" weren't honeymooners, obviously. They were both well-dressed. But her hat wasn't new or her suit, nor were her shoes.

So, as I say, I'd automatically signaled to the bellman to "throw the latch." This is simply a device which makes it easier for employees to keep an eye on suspected parties.

After rooming the couple, the bellman, in closing the door behind him, pushes a tiny button on the inside of the knob handle. This turns a little tumbler inside the lock and makes a black stripe show against the circular center of the latch on the outside. It's inconspicuous enough so as not to be noticed by the guest, but maids, patrols, waiters and bellmen are all trained to watch for them . . . and to report any loud conversations or unusual occurrences which take place behind them.

In "Maurice Wood's" case I heard nothing until the house doctor notified me he'd been called to the room. Mr. "Wood" had been seized with a severe attack of gastric pains. It hadn't been due to anything he'd eaten at the hotel, for though there'd been several room-service calls, they'd all been for liquor. Nevertheless, to safeguard the hotel against any possible lawsuit, the doctor kept me informed about it.

For a couple of hours Mr. "Wood" had been a very

sick man indeed; the doctor had diagnosed it at first as a possible case of *botulinus* poisoning and had been prepared with the proper serum in that event. During the time when the young man was in greatest agony, the secretary had admitted tearfully to the physician that she was not the real wife. She'd suggested that perhaps they ought to phone the home in Jersey, rush the mother of the man's youngsters over from Jersey.

The doctor hadn't thought that would be necessary; he'd taken a chance on that but it had turned out all right. The young man got better; there was no scandal . . . and as far as I know, no divorce. Under those circumstances, naturally, we hadn't attempted any "put-out." Still I was very glad when the couple checked out at noon next day.

Spotting males intent on what police blotters call "disorderly acts" is no problem compared to watching women. Particularly unescorted women.

Women without men are always under surveillance in a hotel; the younger they are the closer they're watched. If they're respectable, they have to be protected against molestation. If they're not, or if they can be considered borderline cases, they're under practically continuous suspicion.

High-grade hotels aren't troubled much with the hardboiled professional hustlers, the regulars who are known to the precinct boys and bail bondsmen. They take their casual clients to cheap rooming houses or "flea-bag" hotels on side streets where the room rates should be, if they aren't, so much per hour instead of per day.

It's the Illegits, the ones you might call the semi-pros, who send house officers to the aspirin bottles. If a couple of them, they often roam around lobbies and cocktail lounges in pairs, order an after-theater snack or a few

57

drinks, the hotel has to serve them just as it does any other guest . . . unless we suspect them of being under age.

During the war, hotels were infested with a whole slew of these bobby-sexers on the make for servicemen. Some of them came from respectable families, but we noticed they always preferred to pick up sailors instead of soldiers or marines. Sailors might have a lot of accumulated pay in their pockets; soldiers seldom did.

I made it a rule around our hotel to keep a strict watch on foot-loose young girls of that sort. We kept moving them down from the mezzanine where they liked to hang out in the hopes of making a date. If they began showing too much stocking in the cocktail lounge I'd send a hostess to tone them down. Eventually they learned that our hotel wasn't a very happy hunting ground and we weren't bothered so much.

But sometimes, especially with young females in the eighteen-to-twenty-two age bracket, it was tough to be sure whether a girl was on the make or just a lonesome party in danger of getting into trouble because of her own amorous impulses. Sometimes one of these girls would be registered as a guest, which gave us a double responsibility: to see that no one bothered *her,* as well as to make sure she wasn't putting anything over. As in the curious case of Miss Hedley.

One Saturday evening around nine, with the lobby fairly empty after the crowds had drifted out to theaters and night spots, I noticed a striking redhead marching briskly to the elevators. I hadn't seen her before. She didn't have that sultry hip-swinging stride which so often marks the streetwalker: as a matter of fact, she looked like a smart young businesswoman. But she kept flicking glances around the lobby out of the corners of her eyes without moving her head to left or right.

I got the notion she was up to something though I'll admit I put her down at first as a possible room-rifler, not a hot number. To discourage any ideas she might have had about getting into some room in the guest's absence, I went up in the elevator with her and let her see that I was giving her the cold eye. It didn't bother her a bit.

She got off at the Fifth. I went up to the Sixth and down the stairs in time to see her letting herself into 564 with a key. That time she *didn't* see me.

Presently I wandered past her door. Two voices, male and female. They weren't making any attempt to keep them low enough not to be heard in the corridor, either. I thought I might have made a mistake about her.

But when I checked with the Rack, 564 was listed as being occupied by a Miss Sue Hedley of New Brunswick, New Jersey.

Now from the hotel's standpoint, it's bad for a male guest—when registered as a single—to have a woman in his room. But a girl who invites men to her room is ten times worse; she can give a house a nasty reputation in no time at all.

So presently I went back up to 564 with an Assistant Manager.

A pleasant feminine voice answered my rap. "Come in." Not, "Who is it?" or "What do you want?" Just, "Come in."

I opened the door; it wasn't locked. The girl in the boudoir chair had her legs crossed to show an interesting amount of hosiery and even a bit of white skin beyond that. She didn't bother to pull her skirts down.

I must have registered astonishment: not at the exposed

59

knees, for neither knees nor legs are a treat to a house officer after some of the things he sees. My surprise was due to the fact that the girl in the chair was a strikingly good-looking brunette.

"Miss Hedley?" I'd told the Assistant Manager she was a redhead; I could tell he was puzzled.

"Yes?" She pulled down her white silk blouse with a sort of stroking gesture which emphasized the bulge of her breasts.

"I'm the house officer."

"No kidding!" She grinned.

"You're not entertaining anyone in your room?" I felt kind of silly asking the question; to tell the truth, I was beginning to wonder if maybe I hadn't gotten off at the wrong floor. But her answer was too much of a wise-crack; it made me sure I wasn't so far wrong.

"Would you expect me to be entertaining a man," batting her eyes demurely, "—sitting down?"

By then the Assistant Manager was convinced I'd made a mistake. "Just wanted to remind you it's against our rules, Miss."

"My goodness, I wouldn't *ever* break one of your old *rules*." She laughed. "But thanks for thinking of me."

She was still laughing when we closed the door. On the way to the Down car, the Assistant Manager wondered how I'd gotten my wires crossed. I had to admit I didn't know.

But I'd thrown the latch myself as I'd left. An hour later I had a call from the Housekeeper's Office. A floor maid had seen the black latch, had heard a man and a woman giggling in 564.

I took the Assistant Manager up again; he must have thought I was building myself up to a mental breakdown but he came along.

This time when we knocked it was a different female voice that called: "Who is it?"

"House officer."

"Just a minute. I'm not dressed."

"We'll wait."

The Assistant Manager whispered: "Not the same girl!"

After three minutes I knocked again. "Give you one more minute, Miss."

The redhead opened the door. She was dressed. The bed was made, but not the way our floormaids are trained to make it up. The ceiling lights were on full; the shade was down. "Yes?" she inquired irritably. "Why did you have to disturb me?"

"Miss Hedley?" I couldn't see any sign of a man or of men's clothing.

"That's right." Blandly. "What do you want?"

"Are you entertaining a gentleman in your room?"

"Not unless you call yourselves gentlemen—crashing in on a girl like this! Would you care to peek under the bed?"

I did that. "Mind if we look in the closet? There's been a report of a sneak thief on this floor, just want to make sure . . ." I didn't wait for her permission, but opened the closet door. Nothing but her coat and a very tiny piece of rawhide luggage.

She sneered. "Don't apologize for rushing away."

I swung the closet door to, the draught it made whipped the window shade back into the room. It was like the curtain going up on a vaudeville stage; on the window sill a pair of tan shoes and blue-trousered legs came into view.

The fellow had raised the bottom half of the window three-quarters of the way, pulled the top half down a couple of inches. He'd crawled out on the sill, reached up and grabbed the top of the upper sash. Then he'd stood up on that narrow stone ledge, six stories above the street, while she'd pulled the shade down to hide him!

He was a scared boy, too. He was mighty glad to have us hang onto him while he scroonched down and climbed back inside the room. All the time we'd been talking to her he'd been trying to keep from staring down dizzily at the sidewalk, nearly a hundred feet below. When we told him he could go, he streaked out of there without so much as a, "So long" to Miss Hedley.

For the redhead really *was* Miss Hedley. She and her brunette chum, Helen, had dreamed up a scheme whereby they could both use the same room for piling up with a number of pickups.

She'd meet a man in the bar, give him the eye, have a drink with him. If he agreed to her price, which was high, she'd give him her room number, go up and leave the door unlocked for him. After she'd "entertained" him, she'd shoo him out, remake the bed and go back to the bar.

By this time Helen would have worked up a little business on *her* account. She'd have some eager prospect panting at the chance to go upstairs with a girl who "never did that sort of thing" but who admitted that "somehow it wouldn't seem wrong with *him*." Sue would slip the key to her unobserved. Helen would go on up and her customer would follow.

Once in a while, for thrills, Sue would rope in some home-blown Casanova, give him the room number and send him up to Helen to be entertained. Or *vice versa*, which I guess is the right term. They really kept those pillows hot.

They worked, they said, only on Saturday afternoons

and evenings. They were stenographers, in a Thirty-eighth Street dress manufacturing firm the rest of the week, had good jobs. Sue claimed the scheme had been worked out because they hadn't wanted to invite men up to the small apartment they shared in the Village; that way there was no danger of any man coming back at some later time when it might have been embarrassing.

Sue, incidentally, told me she was engaged to be married. Had been, after a manner of speaking, laying up a little nest egg, to buy a bedroom suite.

Though it was practically impossible to spot girls like that in the early hours of the evening, since they had none of the characteristics of the regulars, we were pretty well able to keep track of them after midnight. Unescorted women are never very welcome after twelve in a hotel lobby; they're too likely to be propositioned by drunks even if they, themselves, aren't on the make.

Every now and then some palpitating youngster asks me how I can tell whether a woman *is* "on the make." Usually I answer, "Oh, you just get to recognize 'em"— which I'm afraid isn't much help to him if he's looking for a yardstick for his own use.

Truth is, there are a number of things we watch out for without being conscious of looking for them. If a nice but lonesome babe is just feeling bed-conscious, trying to give the eye to some interesting man, she'll give herself away by the way she keeps glancing around the lobby, fixing her hair, calling attention to her legs by pulling down her skirts, so on.

If she's commercially on the make, and this applies to part-time prostitutes, girls with steady jobs and maybe steady husbands, who may go on the loose a couple of times a month to add a few dollars to a slim pay envelope, there'll be suggestive signs about her.

A little too much make-up, a little too much color or flashiness about her clothing. An absence of jewelry aside from a wedding ring, perhaps. It's easier to get a man to part with a sizable sum of money if the girl can plead poverty, which she can't do if she wears pawnable jewelry. Inexpensive handbags, for the same reason. Most of all, a roving eye, not for possible customers only but for house detectives; while professional prostitutes are hardened to arrests and short sentences, the occasional stepper-outer dreads the law like poison.

The expensive call-girl, the kind you've read about in vice trials involving Café Society celebs, bears none of these marks, of course. She generally looks like a show girl or a high-priced cover girl or a slightly hung-over debutante. Very likely she is one or the other.

One thing you can be sure of, you won't see her hanging around a hotel lobby after midnight. She considers her time too valuable to be spent in that fashion.

VII

Saturday Night Panic

LIKE MOST HOTEL MEN, I hate pickpockets. But I will confess to a certain admiration for their dexterity. Directed toward more legitimate channels it might earn them a living as magicians. Matter of fact, the very first pickpocket I ever collared *had* been getting by as a sleight of hand entertainer. Trouble was he couldn't resist the temptation to put on an unadvertised performance in our lobby one evening.

Around the night spots this character was known as Wilhelm the Wizard; at the painless extraction of bill-folds he was certainly that. He'd time his approach to a lobby newsstand so as to come up behind some prosper-ous-appearing party when the latter was on the point of paying for cigars or magazines. As the intended victim put his wallet back in his pocket, Wilhelm would care-lessly chuck a half-dollar on the glass counter. Rather, *at* the counter; he'd toss the coin so it would hit the edge, bounce off onto the carpet.

It's human nature to grab at a dropped coin or at any rate to look for it. Since the coin would fall practically at the prosperous party's feet, he couldn't very well ignore it. He'd stoop to reach for it . . . exposing his wallet— and his gullibility. At the same split second Wilhelm would also bend down. There'd be a collision . . . with the usual mumbling of apologies on both sides. By the time Wilhelm had straightened up and sauntered off, his gain would be the prosperous party's loss.

On the occasion I mentioned, Wilhelm reckoned with-out our blonde cigar-girl. She was just dumb enough not to be misled by the magician's distracting movements or disarming patter; she peered over the counter and asked shrilly what the hell Wilhelm thought he was doing with the prosperous party's billfold. The guest naturally grabbed him. And Wilhelm was so stunned at this fiasco that I had no trouble taking him.

It wasn't usually that easy. Every time I went up against one of these now-you-see-it, now-you-don't boys,

I did it with both hands tied behind my back. I had to do my job without benefit of weapons or authority. It was quite a handicap.

You may get some idea of the setup I faced if you put yourself in the position of an unarmed plain-clothes man in a city of fifty thousand. This is about the number of people circulating in the lobby of a large hotel every week. Let's say you've been stationed at a busy terminal to pick up all suspicious characters. But at the same time, crooks have been tipped off that you don't have a night stick or a gun, not even the right to use your fists.

Suppose, further, that every troublemaker in town is wise you're under instructions not to talk rough or act tough, that you may be verbally abused to any extent without fear of reprisal. How much respect would criminals have for you! That's the spot the house officer is in all the time.

I worked under one other disadvantage as compared to police detectives: I never had any chance to see their lineup of local suspects. Several times a week plain-clothes men in a big city get a good look at every pickpocket arrested in their particular locality; it's a big help. And in place of the daily batch of "flyers" from other police departments, all I had to work with were occasional Warning Bulletins put out by the Hotel Association.

So I had to learn to recognize the members of the brotherhood of the nimble-fingered by what they did rather than by what they looked like.

Every public place is a soft touch for the pickpocket. Hotel bars and lobbies are the softest touch of all. There the leather-lifter doesn't need to sort out the easy marks; they sort themselves out by flashing wads at newsstand, theater-ticket agency or cashier's window. Shrewd eyes note where the leather is replaced, the rest is duck soup for a skilled troupe. Unless the house officer is on his toes.

In hotel bars, especially at rush hours when many customers are crowding in two or three deep to get "just one more quick one" before catching the commuting train or meeting someone for dinner, no one notices the little bump which may mean a missing wallet.

People in hotel lobbies, too, are usually off-guard about their valuables. A woman preoccupied with some other woman's clothes, a man preoccupied with what's inside the other woman's clothes, neither is apt to be alert in regard to purse or pocketbook. He's not likely to catch onto the meaning of those "accidental" bodily contact which are the pickpocket's preparation for an assault by stealth.

And assault is the word for it, since not many of them work solo, as Wilhelm did. Early in the game I discovered most leather-lifters prefer to work in teams; often there's even more ingenuity than dexterity in their methods. There was, for instance, the Injured Innocence act put on by a pair in Boston during my employment at a Tremont Street house there.

They confined operations to our elevators, worked only during check-in and check-out rush hours. I found that the procedure in the Up car went like this:

The male half of the team would step into the car first, standing clear at the back of the car. The girl would wait before getting on, hanging back until some previously selected sucker, a lone man was the best victim, entered the car. Then she'd follow, close on his heels, and turn to stand just in front of him.

When the operator closed the door the victim would be sandwiched snugly between the girl and her partner. The man behind the sucker would quickly reach down as if to fix his shoelace or pull up a sock, to accustom the victim to the idea that any jostling was due to the crowded condition of the car. As the elevator began to rise the male pickpocket would call out "Two" or "Three." and immediately begin to elbow his way toward the front of the car. This, of course, would shove the sucker against the girl's backside. The harder the shove, the better.

Before the operator could get the door open, the girl would squirm around and go into her act, exclaiming indignantly: *"Please* keep your *hands* to yourself!" or whatever might embarrass the helpless sucker.

In the confusion caused by the sucker's drawing back from bodily contact with Miss Injured Innocence, the pickpocket would lift the leather and barge out of the car. He might even give a backward scowl at the sort of lowlife who'd dare make a pass at a nice girl *in an elevator!*

The girl would be glaring resentfully. The redfaced victim would generally be glad to get off the car as quickly as possible, avoiding any exchange of words or glances with Injured Innocence. Seldom did he discover the theft until some time after reaching his room. Even then he frequently failed to connect it with that disagreeable episode in the elevator.

In those cases where a theft was reported, we might get a description of the girl. But somehow we never got the girl.

After a while we caught on; the suckers weren't very careful about the accuracy of the descriptions. Couldn't seem to recall the way she'd been dressed. Evidently their fear of having someone back home hear about her accusation outweighed any chance they might get back their dough.

With variations, that squeeze play is still being worked. We broke it up pretty well by schooling our elevator operators to murmur: "Please watch your valuables, ladies and gentlemen; the management is not responsible in case of loss or theft," whenever any good-looking gal tried to pull the Injured Innocence line on a guest. Possibly some of the feminine protests may have been justified, but then, so was the warning.

Every hotel man knows how important it is to keep vermin out of the hotel; the critters breed . . . and in no time you're overrun with 'em. Same with pickpockets, for an odd reason.

If a room-rifler or a lock-worker gets away with a good score at some hotel, he'll keep quiet about it. He won't brag about it because those crimes are felonies. They mean a stiff jail sentence if anybody should spill to the cops.

But in many cities picking pockets is legally construed as merely taking valuables from a person "without force or duress," which amounts to nothing more than a misdemeanor. This is why the light-fingered brotherhood don't mind bragging about "the terrific take I got away with at the So-and-So hotel tonight."

Let the bunch on the crooked grapevine hear that a man can reef a pocket and make a nice haul at the So-and-so, next thing you know, you're holding a convention for the Amalgamated Leather Lifters. And they're having a field day with your guests.

There are few things which make a guest more unhappy than having to explain to firm or family how somebody stole the money right out of his pants; absolutely nothing more certain to guarantee he'll never come back to the hotel where the theft occurred.

So I always tried to keep one jump ahead of the vermin by training other employees to be on the lookout for them . . . and suggesting where to look. Some of the light-fingered techniques are pretty well known, but it might surprise you to know how often they still put over the old routines.

One setup engineered by troupes of three was called, some years back, Drop the Hanky. I've seen it tried more recently with cigarette cases, compacts, lighters. It was generally worked near the Cashiers' windows, almost always at cocktail time or dinner time, when a lot of people —not all guests, by any means—were crowding up to the grilled wickets to get change or a check cashed.

An attractive cutie would get into line to change a twenty-dollar bill; she'd wave it around so one and all could see it. She'd time her sliding into the queue at the pay-off window so as to edge in just ahead of some middle-aged bird whose clothing suggested a well-padded pocket.

In the line, she'd pretend to be jostled by someone ahead, would contrive to lean back against him, apologize demurely over her shoulder. If he gave her the eye at all, the rest was a cinch.

She'd leave the Cashier's ledge just ahead of him, taking time to stuff change into purse, purse into handbag and so on, while he was completing his transaction. Just as he'd move away from the window, her handkerchief, or nowadays—more likely—her gloves, would fall to the floor.

What could a gentleman do but gallantly stoop to retrieve the bit of cambric? What would such a maneuver do but expose the wallet, into which he'd just stuffed a bunch of lettuce, to the view of any beholder!

The beholder would be the second member of the troupe, sometimes called the "Wire," the man who made the actual contact. He'd have the leather out before the cutie finished murmuring "Thank you *so* much!"

Put this baldly, it may sound crude. It was crude. But if the cutie was attractive enough and the victim sufficiently interested, it often worked like a charm.

In this setup, as in many others, there'd often be a third member of the troupe; this was the one who made it tough on house officers. The third partner in the trio might have been either man or woman; his (or her) function was indicated well enough by the name given this important member of the crew; he was called the "safe."

The instant the "Wire" got his fingers on the leather it was given the hand-is-quicker-than-the-eye treatment, whisked to this receiver.

The actual thief could then loudly protest innocence if he was accused. Usually he would *demand* to be searched on the spot . . . meanwhile breathing fire in the form of threats to sue for false accusation.

I remember one instance where we nabbed both "wire" and "safe" after a scuffle in the cocktail lounge. The "wire" was a young man of twenty or so; the "safe" was his mother. I'd been suspicious of a certain blond who'd been in the queue at the cashier's window twice in the course of an hour. The third time she dropped her compact and had it gallantly retrieved by a bald-headed old boy who looked as if he wished he was presenting her with a mink coat, we closed in on the male member of the team.

We also nabbed the elderly lady to whom the "wire" had passed the bald-head's billfold. We had to take them to the Security Office to search them, of course. The missing wallet, containing close to a thousand in cash, wasn't on either of them. They pretended to be angrily resentful but I could tell they were both laughing at me.

The mother had managed to shuttle that leather back again, right under our eyes, to the charming "shill" . . .

the cutie who pretended to sympathize with the victim over his loss. Unfortunately, she got away before *we* got the picture. Naturally we had nothing on which to base a charge. But anyway I turned them over to the precinct detectives who went around to the "wire's" apartment . . . and picked up the young lady there. There was only a hundred and fifty dollars in the billfold when they nabbed her, though . . . she'd evidently been set to rig up a lopsided split with her boy friend and his mother.

If, in view of the case as I've stated it, it sounds hopeless to keep pickpockets from raiding a hotel's guests ragged, it isn't quite as hopeless as it sounds. The light-fingered crews never work except in crowds, so we know when to expect them. Generally they prefer to go after single men, so we can center our protective efforts somewhat. And by choice, they seem to concentrate their slick tricks around the lobby and the bars, so we know where to be on guard against them.

If you want to know how to spot a leather lifter by his looks, I can't help you. I've known 'em fat, thin, old, young, male, female, sour, genial. The only thing common to all of them, as far as I've noticed—and here I'm talking about the contact man, the "wire"—is that they all seem to have more or less a dead-pan expression. So as not to attract undue attention, I expect.

A lot of the pickpocketing techniques I've heard about aren't attempted in hotels. Such as the boy who breathes garlic in your face on a crowded bus or subway to make you turn your head so he can get into your inside coat pocket, unnoticed. Or the one who crowds up behind you on the train steps or an escalator, then angrily demands that you move up a little to make room for him . . . while he's relieving you of your cash. But there is one almost equally famous method with which, years ago, I had a humiliating experience.

With certain up-to-date refinements, this method is still put into play, expecially on Saturday nights during holiday week ends, when everyone is pretty relaxed and maybe a bit stimulated. It used to be called the Slam and Bang. Nowadays, I understand, it's known as the Panic. The Saturday Night Panic.

It hit Atlantic City while I was still working as a bellman. We had been tipped off that a troupe of Slam-Bang workers were coming down to go through the hotel crowds like a cyclone.

The system this troupe was supposed to employ required that the "shill" carry a suitcase, preferably a heavy one of the black, lacquered metal types then in general use. The "shill" would wade through the crowd, swinging the bag into the shins of some victim . . . *Slam*. The victim would bend over in pain. The "wire" would instantly bump him from behind, lifting the leather in the process . . . *Bang*. The wallet would be handed off to the "safe" in the manner of a T-formation quarterback dealing one off the cuff . . . and the trio was ready for an immediate repeat as the "shill" whammed his way through the crowd.

I made up my mind that if I saw any of that rough stuff, I'd put a stop to it quick enough. All during the afternoon I'd kept a hawk-watch on the few individuals in our lobby who carried their own luggage . . . natural enemies of bellboys, anyhow!

But I saw no one with a metal suitcase until just before five o'clock when I spotted a sorry-looking, underfed individual who seemed to be skulking close to the cashiers' windows. He had a japanned suitcase big enough to have carried a salesman's stock of men's hats.

If the other members of a troupe were lurking near-by, it was clearly my duty to spot them, too. I was so intent on this that I neglected to take my regular turn answering the tap of the desk clerk's bell for "Front boy," thereby passing up a tip or two. But I did jump when a portly individual with a magnificent moustache clamped his hand on my shoulder:

"Boy . . . I've got to catch the five-thirty for North Philly! Hustle up and rush my bags down here." He shoved a key at me; the brass tag read 309. "Get a wiggle on, now. I'll be at the cashier's, paying my bill."

I went up on the double, was back in less than five minutes, met my man at the cashier's, where he was stuffing a receipted bill in his wallet. I helped him lug the bags out . . . and collected a seventy-five cent tip.

In those days a six-bit tip was something to remember. It became something never-to-be-forgotten, shortly after I'd reported back to the Bell Captain's desk.

A tall, skinny man was raising particular ructions at the desk. His pocket had been picked while he was in the bar having a drink or two.

His wallet, which had contained about three hundred dollars, was missing. To add insult to injury, the thief had, at the same time, lifted his room key. Before he could pay for his drinks in the bar he'd have to go up to his room and get some money out of his suitcase. Could he have the duplicate key for Room 309?

I was pretty shamefaced when I owned up to my part in that mess. But it taught me never to accept a person at face value or make snap judgments. The lesson wasn't learned entirely at the other fellow's expense, either.

The management docked me three dollars a week out of my slim pay, as my share for what the portly party had cost them in repaying the guest. I didn't feel too badly about it; if they meant to keep me on until it was all paid, I thought, I didn't need to worry about getting fired for quite a while.

VIII

Those Gay Nighties

IF THE NETWORKS ever get the notion of putting a house detective's experiences on the air, I can suggest a title which would fit like the fat girl's corset: *Sex Can Be Dangerous.*

After eagle-eyeing lobbies and patrolling plush-carpet beats for years you'd think nothing along that line could astonish a house officer. You'd be wrong. I kept right on being surprised up to the day I quit. That crack about "What won't some people think up next!" gets worked to death around a Security Office.

Take, for instance, that "orgy" which was supposed to have been staged in the hotel where I was Chief a year or so before I retired. I wouldn't have called it an orgy myself, though that's what the tabs labeled it. You may recall those headlines; the real facts were a bit different than the story which hit the front pages.

One Saturday afternoon around six-thirty, early in April, I was conning our cram-packed lobby for whizz workers or bag-snatchers when suddenly I got the H.O. sign from the Bell Captain's desk: the three quick flashes of the little green light which says Hurry Over.

When I got through the crowd the captain on duty

pointed toward our street entrance: "Some commotion outside, Mister Collans. Kong just gave me the office; he's out there now."

Kong was the nickname for our outsize Lithuanian doorman. He was six foot seven and so wide he had to squeeze through the revolving door edgeways; naturally he had to be called King Kong, Kong for short. In addition to having to buy shirts that would have fitted a grizzly he was, for a doorman, a pretty smart apple. I knew he wouldn't have called me outdoors at peak rush unless there was urgent need of it.

On the way out I picked up Bill, one of my lobby assistants; we went down the steps to the street level, fast.

As we hit the door, four sailors in dress whites came piling in, all with wide grins pasted across their faces. They weren't drunk or boisterous; they just seemed in a terrific swivet to get somewhere in a hurry. A lot of servicemen were in the habit of meeting their gal-pals in our lobby so neither Bill nor I saw anything out of the ordinary in that.

Once on the street, we saw a crowd milling around in front of the drugstore which occupied the corner of our ground floor. There didn't seem to be any fracas, but at the core of the gathering a couple of sailors were exhibiting a pair of blue nylon step-ins. Each had a grip on part of the flimsy garment; they were trying to harmonize on *Never Trust A Sai-lor An Inch A-bove The Knee* . . .

There was no sign of Kong.

Bill asked one of the bystanders if he'd seen the doorman.

"Big lunk?" The man laughed and leered. "Yeah, he's in the drugstore. He tried t' get them panties away from the gobs—they hung a shiner on him! Oh, a beaut!"

It was about the time when every newspaper carried a

76

new story about pantie raids at some college dormitory or sorority house; the crowd evidently figured this was just one of those things.

I sent Bill into the drugstore, waded through the crowd toward the sailors. Before I reached them they spotted me as some kind of authority. One of them, a little banty, stuck his chin out belligerently:

"Lookin' for sump'n, Mac?"

I asked what all the excitement was about.

"No excitement," the other sniggered. "None whatever. We ain't the kind to get excited over a dame's pants, are we, keed?" He flapped the step-ins in a burlesque of a bullfighter's gesture.

The crowd roared appreciation.

The pair began an off-key duet to *Those Old Red Flannel Drawers That Maggie-e-e-e-e Wore.*

Bill tore out of the drugstore, wigwagging frantically.

He pointed straight up. I began to get it. That piece of lingerie had come from one of our rooms. Probably Kong had seen it flutter to the sidewalk, tried to recover it, been socked by the sailors who'd decided it was finders keepers.

I hadn't guessed the half of it. Bill gave it to me on the run:

"Girls up on the ninth or tenth, Dev. Began chucking their lingerie out the windows . . . just raising hell, I guess. Kong saw the stuff come floatin' down . . . heard some of the sailors holler: *Lookit! They's a room number on this one, in lipstick!* Then another grabs the pair Kong has, belts him a good one. All the time th' sailor's yowling to his pals—'*Hey! This babe writes "C'monup'n see me, sometime!"*' Know what I think? That bunch that busted in when we come out,—they'll be upstairs in that room by now!"

I thought he was right. We didn't bother with the singers; we hustled back inside. As we went up in the service car, Bill told me Kong was getting stuff put on a cut eye so the blood wouldn't get on his uniform.

Without waiting to round up one of the Assistant Managers, Bill and I raced to the 941-943 suite. I'd remembered a group of girls from a Southern college had checked in on the ninth the previous night, four sharing that corner suite.

Sounds of revelry were coming from 941, all right. Loud masculine voices and shrill feminine squeals quieted down soon as I rapped on the door.

For a minute or so they pretended not to hear us. When I announced we were coming in with my key unless they opened up, the quartette of sailors began to talk tough.

"You bust in here, dickie bird, you'll *get* busted!"

"Come on in; we got somep'n *for* you!"

In a case like that there's only one thing to do. Bill used his key on the 941 door. I went in 943. Making a double entry that way, the sailors weren't sure how many of us there were, so they didn't start anything. The girls were hanging onto them, anyway, to prevent any battle royal.

There were six girls. One was locked in the bathroom with a sailor. She made him open the door when she heard us in the room. All she was wearing was a negligee you could read a newspaper through. The other girls all had bathrobes or dressing gowns on, not much else. They were lookers, every one. None of them were really intoxicated but they'd all been drinking bourbon. So had the sailors, by that time . . . and *they* hadn't needed any extra stimulation to begin with. One of the boys kept trying to nibble his girl's neck even after I'd come into the room.

78

I used the phone on the table of the suite's living room. "Collans in 941, Emergency. Rush three, four men up here, *pronto*. Call the Shore Patrol. Get them over here. Snap it up."

The boys were sore at having their wonderful party broken up. Two of them began to rough Bill around. I didn't go to his assistance; the last thing in the world we wanted was a free-for-all.

Bill played it right. He kept his hands to himself, took a few shoves in the chest, all the time treating it as a big joke: "You fellows better beat it before that Shore Patrol runs you in . . . They'd slap you in for duration, they caught you like this. You haven't much time if you want to stay out of the jug . . ."

I kept moving around so the others couldn't corner me. "You wouldn't want to get these nice girls in a jam, now?" I asked them quietly. "You boys are too regular to want to see these kids hauled into court, get their mothers and fathers mixed up in this mess. You call it a day, before you make a lot of trouble. You can wait down in the lobby if the girls want to meet you later."

Some of the Navy wanted to slug it out with us but finally we shooed them all outside. Then we got hold of the house doctor and his nurse, to make sure the girls really were all right. Of course the girls claimed "nothing had happened," still we had to be sure.

Meantime, I cancelled the Shore Patrol call and got in touch with one of our hospitality hostesses and the resident manager's secretary, who lived in the hotel. They came up and played housemother to those kids. The girls had started the whole thing as a gag, never intending the sailors to come up to the room. Then one of the girls, on a dare, had scribbled the room number on her underwear, tossed it to the waiting wolves.

79

When the sailors arrived, the sextette thought it would be fun to give the boys a thrill. Nothing more than a thrill, they agreed.

All that actually happened was some high-voltage necking. Of course the papers called it a Juvenile Orgy. It might have been, at that, if we hadn't been on the job and lucky.

One thing sure, sex is certainly more of a problem for hotels than it used to be. Maybe there isn't any more of it than there used to be, but it's handled more casually. War-time habits are partly to blame; from what I've learned I'd say that among young men in the services any tendency toward *not* being promiscuous is scorned as sissy.

Post-War tensions have their effect on girls, too. What is sometimes referred to as "sleeping around" has become so general that one of our court clinics has had to set up an official definition:

A promiscuous woman is any married woman who has engaged in extramarital relationships within the last six months or any single woman who has had sexual relations with more than one man or with one man more than twice, within the same period.

On that basis, most hotels cater, whether knowingly or not, to promiscuity all the time. Matter of plain fact, that isn't so great a problem to a house officer. He can't spend his time asking couples for photostats of licenses or inspecting wedding rings to see whether they came from Tiffany's or the five-and-dime. He can't operate on a basis of morality; it comes down to a matter of appearance and behavior.

The plain truth is that if you are, say, over twenty-five and you and your companion are well-dressed and decently mannered, nobody is likely to question you when you check in at a good hotel, whether or not you have gone through a ceremony with the right kind of license. Security men have to concentrate on the sex angles which annoy and disturb others or which may in some way hurt the hotel's reputation.

In my experience, the most common of these is the individual who lets his lustful instincts run berserk the minute he's in a hotel room in some strange city.

People who go on the prowl in bars or night clubs or dance halls for sexual adventure are no problem unless they try to bring their pickup partners up to their rooms. The lad we have to be on the lookout for is the one who can't take his sex or leave it alone; the type who starts on a sex spree the minute he checks in.

This person may lack confidence in his ability to find what he's looking for, in competition with others at bars and places of entertainment. Or he may just be in too much of a tizzy to wait. In either case he is likely to make advances toward some of the hotel staff.

Here are a few examples (and I haven't been too careful about disguising them because somehow I don't think they'll sue me for slander) from file cards I kept on people of this sort:

A. H. T——. Retired manufacturer from Indiana. Age 62. Married. Dignified, might be professor or minister. *Complaint:* Called floormaid for extra bath towels; when she brought them he pranced around the room naked in front of her. Offered her money, etc. Admitted acts, on investigation.

B. K. W——. Mech. engineer, 38, home, T——, Okla. Single. Called public stenographer to dictate tech. reports. While doing so put hands on her person, kissed her, offered money for intimacies. Denied, on investigation.

C. M. A——. This girl, 19 yrs. old, cashier in chain market, S——, Georgia, staying at hotel to see rel. off to Europe. After ordering bkfast from roomservice, she had waiter set up table close to bedside, then threw back covers, got out of bed, wearing only top half of pajamas. Asked waiter if he didn't think she had nice-looking legs, etc. Denied, on investigation.

D. T. K——. Sales rep., bag company. Made offers of large sums to phone operator on hotel PBX if she would come to his room after going off shift. Failing in this, offered money if she would connect him with "some good hot number" in hotel. Used indecent language. Was intox. when investigated. Partial admission, dismissed.

E. Mrs. F. D——. Age 53, widow, lives M——, Tenn., buyer for ret. store. Called bellman Y——, 10:15 for cigarettes; on deliv. same he found her in shower where she wanted cigs delivered. She stepped out of shower, asked Y—— to rub back with towel, etc. On his refusal, she became abusive, threatening to tell manager Y—— tried to rape her. Denial and counter accusation on investigation.

These weren't exceptional cases. Any Security man could find dozens like them in his records if he's been in protection work very long. I'm sure most house officers will agree when I say that handling matters of this sort is as tricky as juggling broken bottles.

Generally there's no evidence except the unsupported word of the hotel's employee. No crime has been committed, and the house detective doesn't have authority to do a thing about it, anyhow. So my procedure was, ordinarily, to go to the guest's room with an Assistant Manager, never taking the complainant along.

I would make a respectful report of the complaint, being careful to word it so it wouldn't be a direct accusation. Sometimes the guest would admit his mistake. In such cases often there'd be an attempt to hand a few dollars to the house officer and sometimes to the Assistant Manager in the hope they would hush the matter up. The guest wouldn't be aware how much the hotel wanted to keep the whole business quiet, anyway.

Once in a while a guest who admitted he'd been caught with his passions down would become remorseful, tearful and on rare occasions would try, or fake, a suicide attempt. I always made sure the house doctor was in the room before I left, in those instances.

The usual result of an investigation was an indignant denial, many times accompanied by violent abuse. I've had the vice-president of an important electrical firm try to knock my teeth out because I reported to him that an elevator operator had complained of repeated lewd caresses and fumblings.

A quiet-looking woman of thirty, a music teacher from Vermont, who'd done her best to seduce a manicurist she'd called to her room once threw a sherry bottle at the head of the Assistant Manager who was in the room with me at the time. Immediately afterward she threatened to set fire to the hotel. We got her out with no delay, believe me.

Where the abuse was only verbal, we had to take it, with no comeback. The denials were always accepted with cold skepticism and the guest allowed to remain. But no matter how wrathfully indignant they had been, no matter how loudly they had protested their innocence, they invariably checked out the next morning as if in retaliation for being wrongfully accused.

There are two reasons for checking up on all complaints of a sex nature. The first is to beat the guest to the punch in case he, or she, decides on a counter-complaint or on other means of retaliation. The second is that any guest who thinks he can pull raw stuff and get away with it will keep on trying, maybe with more success.

In any large hotel where thousands of men and women are employed, some of them temporarily or on part time, there are bound to be a few who'll play pat-a-cake with guests for money. If a guest should make contact with one of these, there may be trouble with a delayed take.

An undergraduate in California once sued a chain, in one of whose hotels I worked, for heavy damages as the aftermath of a brief bed-down with one of the floormaids in its Cleveland unit. He claimed the hotel had been grossly negligent in employing a female infected with venereal disease.

An unmarried floormaid sued a Boston hotel, with which I had been connected, for doctor and hospital fees as a result of giving birth to an illegitimate child "conceived while plaintiff was engaged in her regular duties as an employee." The name of the guest presumed to be the papa wasn't given in the bill of particulars so I suppose she never knew his name. Possibly the baby was merely given a room number.

Hotels now have stricter rules covering the presence of female employees in the rooms of male guests. When possible the maids work in pairs. The Housekeeper makes frequent and irregular tours of inspection on the floors. Doors are required to be left open at all times the maid is in a guest's room. These regulations make it difficult for employees to get away with shenanigans, but to rephrase the oldie, "Sex will find a way," and there'll always be a few employees who'll risk losing their jobs for cash in hand.

By and large, though, it's my experience that the moral standards of hotel people are higher than that of the guests they serve. If this weren't true, the Security Office wouldn't get much help from employees in keeping the establishment clean and decent. Whereas actually the maids, housekeepers, room-service waiters, bellmen, etc. are the eyes and ears of the house officers. Especially floormaids.

They notice lipstick stains on tissues in the wastebaskets of single male guests. A bobby pin on the floor beside the bed, a long blonde hair on the edge of the washbasin, powder on the glass top of the bureau, an odor of perfume near the closet. Or cigar ashes in the room of a female Single.

The case of Mrs. Ayar (as I'll call her) shows how much help an alert floormaid can be. Mrs. Ayar was a kittenish-mannered redhead with a nice figure even if she was in her late thirties. She was married to a well-to-do rug retailer who brought her along to New York to attend a convention held at our hotel. As many others in his trade association did, he took a room on the third floor to be near the sample exhibits and conference rooms.

He was a rolypoly butterball of a man who seemed jealously fond of his wife. He dressed her and decorated her as if she lived in a showcase. She might have, from his point of view. She was his most convincing display of success in his line of business, always loaded down with rings, pins, necklaces and a fine emerald-studded bracelet.

During the week she stopped at our hotel she seemed to enjoy meeting and mingling with the men and women in her husband's trade association. Evidently she felt it was up to her to be a good mixer on his account. She was constantly wandering in and out of the sample showrooms, saying "Hi" to people she didn't know, being nice to everybody.

Afternoons there was always someone around to offer her a drink; generally she took it, and she seemed to handle it all right. Toward the end of the week, while Mr. Ayar was busy in the committee rooms, Mrs. Ayar stuck pretty close to the third floor instead of roaming around sight-seeing like many of the other wives.

On the last afternoon of the convention, while Mr. Ayar was occupied with some Association business, Mrs. Ayar bumped into a handsomely distinguished gentleman in the corridor. Literally bumped into him, or so she thought, for she spilled one of the two highballs he was carrying. She apologized prettily. He smiled amiably. After a few moments they were talking together like old friends.

She couldn't remember having met the distinguished gentleman though he gallantly made it clear *he* hadn't forgotten *her*. He'd been *so* impressed with her the minute he'd seen her, the evening before. Mrs. Ayar had been pretty well stimulated the night before at the big banquet; her recollection of people was a bit vague. But after he'd identified himself as Charlie Graysett, a prominent linoleum jobber, she sort of thought maybe she *did* remember him.

She accepted the unspilled highball while he suggested their stepping down the hall to his room while he got a refill.

Mrs. Ayar thought there'd be no harm in that. Her husband would be tied up with his old committee work for another hour or so. How could she spend the time more agreeably than by chatting with this interesting gentleman; perhaps the friendship might later be of use to her husband.

86

She'd been in and out of a dozen rooms on that floor during the week; going to Graysett's room would be no different, she thought, than visiting any of the others in which numdahs, druggets, domestic Orientals and so on were exhibited.

He led her around a bend in the corridor, to its far end. As soon as she'd stepped into his room she saw there were no samples of floor coverings to be seen. It was merely a man's bedroom, with bottles, glasses and a bowl of ice as the only display.

Immediately she felt uneasy. It wasn't right for a lady to be alone with a man in his bedroom . . . and the door locked, too! That locking of the door frightened her. She decided she didn't want a drink. She wanted out. She said so.

But Graysett slid his arm around her waist, held her, began to let his hands wander. She resisted. He pulled her toward the bed, wrestled her onto it. She struggled. Her clothes began to be disarrayed. She became more frightened, warned him she'd scream unless he released her instantly.

She didn't scream. Right then, as if on cue, the door burst open, a brassy blonde rushed in. The blonde was evidently Mrs. Graysett. The newcomer was furious, raging at the man as a treacherous louse and a dirty deceiver. But she went at Mrs. Ayar tooth and nail.

She howled that she'd fix the bitch who was trying to steal her husband! Piled up on the bed like that with her skirts up around her neck! She'd call the cops, have this little tramp of a redhead sent to jail!

Whatever fear Mrs. Ayar had experienced earlier in the amorous clutches of Graysett were nothing compared to her terror at this unexpected assault. Suppose the po-

87

lice should be called in! What would her husband think? What *could* he think!

Mrs. Graysett raved on: she'd sue for alienation of affections. She'd take every penny this "other woman" had to her name, strip her of all that jewelry . . . which probably had been given to Mrs. Ayar by Graysett, anyhow.

That gave Mrs. Ayar a desperate idea, as it was intended to. She tore off her emerald bracelet, offered it to the "wife" if she'd only forget the wretched affair.

The blonde laughed in her face. She wouldn't settle for any bracelet, she was going to phone the police right then.

Mrs. Ayar was stripping off her rings to add them to the bracelet when I came into the picture.

One of our late-shift floormaids had wheeled her linen cart into the third floor corridor at just the moment Graysett was locking his door, after following Mrs. Ayar into the room. The maid had paid no attention until, after the door had closed, the blonde hurried down the corridor, stood outside Graysett's door listening. The blonde had made the mistake of having her room key out, ready to use . . . but not using it.

Ordinarily, guests don't stand listening outside their rooms with keys poised for a quick entrance. The maid let herself into an unoccupied room, notified her assistant housekeeper who passed the tip along to me.

If that maid hadn't been on her toes, in another five minutes "Mr. and Mrs. Graysett" would have been out of the hotel. And silly little Mrs. Ayar would have had a bad time trying to explain to her husband what had happened to eight or ten thousand dollars worth of jewelry.

We didn't press charges, to save Mrs. Ayar's . . . and her husband's . . . feelings. As far as I know, he never learned of the matter. But about a month after the Ayars had gone back to the Middle West I received a small, insured package in my mail. In it was a wristwatch engraved:

To Devlin Collans
With Eternal Gratitude

There was no card or note with the gift. So I never wrote to Mrs. Ayar to thank her. But it was a good watch. I still wear it.

IX

None of That Here

THE STATLER CHAIN spent years and millions to impress on its employees, and on the public, that its houses are operated on the principle: The Guest Is Always Right. I always modified that maxim, myself.

I'd go so far as to admit the guest should be considered Right when he honestly *thought* he was. The distinction covers a lot of ground. There are plenty of times when a guest won't even *claim* he's Right. Here are a few out of my collection of Wrongoes.

The drunk who, after being talked out of starting a snake dance in the lobby to celebrate his alma mammy's victory, grabbed the controls away from our elevator operator and zoomed a carful of frightened people ten stories skyward before the operator could take over again.

The guest who enjoyed his stay with us in a cognac-colored haze but who decided, when presented with the bill for his smörgäsbord and room, that he was being robbed and thereupon dug down in his pocket for all the coins he had, flung them into the face of the girl cashier with the yell: "Take it all, you lousy burglars—take my last cent!"

The bird who thought it was great fun, from his ringside table beside the dance floor in the grill, to roll empty club-soda bottles out among the dancers, howling with mirth whenever a girl tripped on one or stumbled and fell.

The young lady who had the original idea of livening up a dull party by sticking her head out a ninth-floor window one hot August night and screaming "Fire! Fire!" at the top of her lungs.

The middle-aged gentleman with the distinguished ambassadorial beard (I never did find out what he did, besides play Life-of-the-Party) who came down to our lobby in full formal dress except for his shoes and stockings, evidently under the impression he'd been tapped as a zany by the *Truth or Consequences* radio show. He caused quite a commotion by brandishing a pair of scissors and stepping up to every available lady to inquire in the most polite manner if he might snip off a small piece of her girdle.

The stout woman who bitterly contested the maid's right to come in and clean up her room, insisting she only wanted her bed linen changed once a week. She stayed in her room all the time. Her room-service waiter reported she wore a bath towel tied around her head covering the right side of her face, insisting she had a terrible toothache. But the steaks she ordered every evening didn't match up with the toothache excuse, so eventually I had to check up on her.

She refused point-blank to let me and our Assistant

Manager in or even to open the door. We notified the phone operator not to accept any more calls from her room; as soon as she found out she couldn't get anything to eat, she checked out in a great hurry.

I saw her photograph in one of the tabloids a week or so later; she was a trained nurse from Omaha who'd been indicted in an Abortion Ring and was hoping to hide out in New York until things cooled down. They'd picked her up in an Automat, gorging on a tray loaded with ice cream and pastry.

Any house officer could add dozens of examples of his own; a good share of the nuisances would be either drunks or practical jokers or both. Practical jokers were a serious problem since there was always a danger of someone's getting hurt, in which case there'd sometimes be an attempt to call it an accident due to some negligence of the hotel or its staff.

I've had a man tell me with a perfectly straight face that he broke his ankle getting out of the bathtub, due to a defective hand bar, when I knew perfectly well, from the condition of the room, that he'd been a victim of his friends' horseplay. Probably it was the old schoolboy trick of having Conspirator A drop on hands and knees behind him while Conspirator B gave him a healthy shove. In any case I merely had to point out that the ridges showing on the skin of his foot, left by his ribbed sock, were still visible . . . which they wouldn't have been after a tub bath.

Once in a while I'd be called in to smooth down the ruffled feathers of some guest who'd been made a patsy by his pals. Mrs. Carter Bersing was such a sufferer.

I was leaning over the mezzanine railing one afternoon when the sound of voices raised in anger made me look over at the registration desk. A young and pretty woman, smartly dressed in a white linen suit, was alternately bawling out her husband and the room clerk. I could tell that Arny, our desk man, was being apologetic and it was plain the young woman's husband was trying to talk his way out of something . . . with no success.

By the time I got down there everyone in the lobby was watching them. The young lady was screaming with rage, her husband was trying to quiet her while looking as if he'd liked to do it with his hands around her throat.

It didn't take long to discover that Mrs. J. Carter Bersing—that was the way the register read, *Mr. and Mrs. J. Carter Bersing, Willimantic, Conn.,* was accusing her husband of having been unfaithful to her "right here in this same hotel" only a couple of days before.

Arny explained: "All my fault, Mrs. Bersing . . . just a mistake, I assure you, it is. I never saw Mr. Bersing before in my life. If you doubt my word, or his, ask Mister Collans, here. He's our Chief Security Officer, he'd be sure to remember if this gentleman had been staying here recently."

I said I'd never seen the gentleman before to the best of my recollection, certainly not recently.

The young lady wasn't mollified one bit. "Naturally, you men all stand up for each other. You *did* ask my husband if he wanted the same room he had last week, *didn't you?*"

Arny, red in the face, admitted he had, but that it had been simply one of those errors you were likely to make when you saw so many people, face to face. He looked appealingly at me, to help him out of a hole.

J. Carter wasn't willing to let Arny off so easy; the husband was on the hook and he knew such a denial wasn't going to get him off it. *He* demanded to know why Arny had pulled a blooper like that.

I took Mr. Bersing's side, suggesting that he and his wife step into the Credit Manager's office for a moment, probably the whole thing could be straightened out.

Her husband's attitude must have had a sobering effect on the young lady because she came along, still mad as she could be, but not screaming.

I went back to Arny. He had his excuse in his hand: a card from the Rack of three days previous: *Mr. and Mrs. J. Carter Bersing, Willimantic, Conn.* Room 1711.

"I remembered the name, Dev. . . . I hadn't seen the guy . . . that was my day off, but I always look the cards over next morning when I come on duty, to see if anyone I know's come in the house. You couldn't forget a name like J. Carter Bersing, so naturally when I saw it on that registration card a few minutes ago I tried to make like I was welcoming him back to the house again, by asking if he wanted the same room he and Mrs. Bersing had occupied before. So she goes white as a sheet and pushes him away from her with some crack about 'So *this* is where you were last week!'"

I told him to dig up the original registration card for the earlier date. Then I signaled to the bell captain, told him to check back on his ledger, find the bellman who'd checked the party into 1711, send him to me at the Credit Office.

When Arny brought me the original registration it was easy to tell a different person had written the name J. Carter Bersing: the name was easier to read, as if the signer had been taking great care to make sure it was legible—or as if the signer wasn't used to writing the name.

I took the card to the Credit Office, laid it in front of Mrs. Bersing. "Someone who must have known you and your husband were coming here played a little joke on you, Mrs. Bersing." Then I asked him if he recognized the handwriting.

He studied it with his forehead all puckered up.

The bellman came to the door: "You want me, Mister Collans?"

I asked him if he remembered rooming Mr. and Mrs. Bersing in 1711, a few days before.

Sure, he did.

What did the gentleman look like?

"He was short and kind of plump-like, not exactly fat I guess but on the heavy side, with kind of curly blond—"

"Mike!" It was a chorus from J. Carter and Mrs. Bersing. They stared at each other a second. Then he began to laugh . . . and she, woman-like, began to bawl.

She was so *terribly* sorry she'd accused him!

He roared he'd break Mike's Goddamned neck when they got back home!

She wondered if he could forgive her for having such a nasty, suspicious mind . . .

They carried on like that for a minute while the bellman looked puzzled and I doped out that Mike was a neighbor of the Bersings and worked for the same company as J. Carter.

The pay-off, though, was when Bersing broke into his wife's protestations with a "Say!"

"What?" she asked.

"Mr. and *Mrs.*" he raised his eyebrows as he tapped the card on the desk.

"Oh!" she gasped. "I never *thought! Mike's not married!!*"

The joke was on the hotel, after all.

But for every other variety of nuisance, there were ten difficult drunks to handle. And being bouncer for a high-grade hotel is by no means the cinch you might expect it to be.

It's much tougher than being the heave-o specialist in a bar or café. One reason is that proprietors of most such places will put up with a lot more than a good hotel can stand . . . and maintain its reputation.

In some bars a dispute or even a fight isn't exactly discouraged, at least not until broken glass begins to fly or someone starts to thumb a spring blade. Even in places where the attitude is more strict, the bouncer can grab the offender by the collar and give him the bum's rush to the street door. You couldn't do that in a good hotel. A house officer had to do his ejecting with tact instead of force, unless it was an extreme emergency . . . and then we'd prefer to let the police take over, if possible.

Waiters and barmen took care of pass-out drunks whenever possible. If rubbing ice on the back of the intoxicated party's neck didn't bring him around, the helpless individual was simply carried out. If, as was usually the case, there was someone with him, we'd load the drunk in a cab and let the friend take it from there. If he'd been alone, he was generally put in a bedroom near the hospital suite so the house doctor could take a look at him every now and then.

But when it came to the belligerent buckos, there'd be a H.O. call. If the drunk was in the lobby and merely at the vocal stage, I'd ask him to take it easy, tone it down a bit. If he raised the tempo, out of resentment, I'd ask if he was a registered guest; if so, I'd have to ask him to go to his room . . . or check out. Sometimes the check-out suggestion would quiet him, if he wasn't too far gone to realize he'd have trouble getting in any other hotel . . . of course no first-class house will room an obviously intoxicated person.

When the drunk was trying to pick a fight, the first step was to give him a warning as much in the manner of a cop as possible. I'd try to step between the two quarreling individuals with a quiet "None of that here, gentlemen." If both of the belligerents were intoxicated, I worked on the one I thought was the least out of control, even though he might have been the most pugnacious.

Often he'd switch his anger to me, cursing me or maybe taking a poke at me. I might have to ward off a punch, but I never swung back at him . . . *in the hotel.* If I could see no chance of quieting him down, I'd pretend to get sore at some crack he'd made and come back with: "You haven't guts enough to come out on the sidewalk and say that!" Often he did have; the rest was easy.

If I couldn't handle him, our doorman was there to lend a hand or blow his whistle in the three short blasts which is a signal for help in police language everywhere.

If a fight had started before I got to the spot I always grabbed the nearest hotel employee—bellman, porter, Assistant Manager, elevator man—to help me. I'd grasp the arm of one of the battlers, swinging him around so he couldn't see the fellow at whom he'd been slugging, while the other employee would do the same to his opponent. It was surprising how quickly a pugnacious person would cool off if he couldn't get a good look at the guy whose block he'd been trying to knock off a few seconds before.

When the H.O. call came from the bar, it was a tougher nut to crack. I don't pretend to know the psychological quirks which cause it, but it's a fact that nearly everyone at a bar is "agin" the house officer when he's called to remonstrate with a drunk. This has been true, in my experience, even when the drunk has been causing discomfort and embarrassment to those around him, the only exception being in the case of the drunk who has been shooting off four-letter words in the presence of ladies.

I always tried to take advantage of this apparently automatic resentment by getting the drunk to center his wrath on me, accepting his abuse, conning him along. Many times his wrath has been roused, in the first place, because his girl or one of his companions or possibly the bartender, had suggested he'd had all he could handle. That seems to infuriate a certain type of drinker, who guesses *he* knows, by God, when he's had enough!

Once in a while I'd even buy such a stew "one more," on his faithful promise to leave after that nightcap. I always found that an appeal to an intoxicated person's "honor"—even when it was apparent he was in no condition to know up from down—was more effective than any attempt at reasoning with him.

Occasionally a little corny humor would get a tough-talking drunk to calm down. We had one guest at the hotel where I worked during the early forties, who got well potted every Saturday night he stayed with us, and he came up from Washington every couple of weeks. Like most rough-and-ready customers he was a small man but he had been, he boasted, a champion in the lightweight division while he was in college. It could have been true.

One Saturday night when he'd gotten around to his usual combative stage of announcing that he might not be the biggest guy in the bar but, by God, he could lick any man around, I asked him if he really meant that challenge.

He squinted at me. "Cer'n'ly, meant it."

"All right," I told him, "there's one bird out in the lobby who'll take you up."

He followed me out of the bar, much to the relief of our head barman. Several of the Washington man's drinking companions tagged along to see the outcome.

When I led him to the elevator and said: "There's the fellow who'll take you up," his pals began to pound each other on the back and roar with laughter. The elevator man was a tall skinnymarink with very little meat on him. The drunk decided not to be a bad sport about it, stepped into the car and waved goodnight. "Know when I'm licked," he muttered.

The elevator man was a little uneasy, but when he came down he showed me a dollar bill. "This is getting to be a good job, Mister Collans. I'm makin' side-money now."

Not all of them were as easy as that, of course. I've had drunks take good solid punches at me, without being able to sock back. I've had the same men call up next day and apologize, too.

Only once did I get into a real knockdown and drag-out, for which I had no one to blame but myself. One winter night around half-past ten—this was at the Boston hotel where I'd probably have stayed forever if my wife hadn't wanted to get back to New York—a young woman came in without any baggage, went hurriedly to the registration desk.

She was quietly dressed and not too breezily mannered, but she seemed to be having some trouble with the desk clerk, so I drifted over where I could hear. He'd asked her for the price of the room in advance, since she didn't have any luggage. She didn't have enough money but had offered to stop in the next day and pay for the room; she just *couldn't* go home.

When I got a good look at her, I could guess why. Her thin and rather sad face was disfigured by a black eye. I asked her about it.

Yes, she admitted, her husband had given it to her; she'd been afraid to stay in the house with him because he'd threatened to beat her up. He was ordinarily, she said, a good man, but a holy terror when drunk.

If we couldn't trust her for the room, could we let her sleep in one of the lobby chairs till morning? She could go home by morning; he'd be sober then . . .

Of course we couldn't have her sitting around the lobby all night, so I okayed the registration. She repeated her promise to come in and pay next day. After she'd gone up to bed, I had that inner glow you get from doing a good deed in a naughty world . . . you hope.

The hope wasn't quite justified. Apparently, after she'd gone upstairs, the girl had become worried that her man might have fallen asleep smoking and set the house on fire. So she used the room phone to ring up a neighbor who lived in the apartment across the hall from them, asked her to look in and see if the husband was all right. Just in case there should have been anything very wrong to report, our overnight guest mentioned the hotel where she'd taken refuge.

First thing I knew of all this was when a great big hulk-shouldered bruiser lurched in off the street with blood in his eye and a breath that could have been bonded. He demanded to know what room his wife was staying in.

When nobody would tell him, he started throwing things at the desk clerk, the "front" bell, the bronze name plate of the Clerk On Duty.

I went for him. He was delighted to have the chance to mop up the lobby with me. He was very drunk and probably clumsy even when sober, but if one of his roundhouse rights had connected, it would have been curtains for Collans. It was fairly exciting for a few minutes.

But when I finally got him out in the street, there were

two shiners in that family. She didn't think badly of me for fixing him up the same as he'd fixed her, either.

Because next day when she came in to pay her bill, she told me he'd gone to the priest and taken the pledge . . . on the theory that if any little shrimp like that house detective could lick him when he was drunk, it was time for him to stay sober.

X

The Switchover Swindle

FOR MANY YEARS house detectives in films were a composite of Keystone comedy cops and Jimmy Cagney toughs—pictures typed the house officer as a poker-faced joker wearing a hard-boiled hat, a suspicious scowl and a well-gnawed cigar butt. That unflattering caricature, I'm glad to say, is being replaced by a more complimentary one, both in movies and on the printed page. Trouble is, the new stereotype, the super Sherlock, is almost as far removed from the truth as the old comic version.

There may be some Security Officers who can, as this new stereotype suggests, size up a guest in a second, cataloguing the essential facts about him with the speed of a punch-card machine. I'll admit *I* can't glance at an incoming guest and tell how much money he has, what model car he drives and whether his intentions in obtaining a room for himself and blonde are strictly honorable or otherwise. Still, there's enough truth in this new picture of the Security Officer to make it plausible.

It might startle you to learn just how much the Security Staff of an up-to-date hotel *can* find out about a guest if it wants to. Point is, of course, in most cases it doesn't want to. If you're quiet and reasonably well-behaved you can spend a month in any good hotel, without having anyone in the least interested in finding out your occupation, your marital status or your amorous intentions.

On the other hand, if there's anything offbeat about your appearance, behavior or belongings, then you'll attract plenty of attention from the Security Office. However, even then there'll be no dependence on Sherlock-type deductions or miraculous guesswork. What the hotel finds out about you will come as the result of teamwork between various employees. The case of Harold M—— will show what I mean.

Mr. M—— crossed my path a couple years ago while I was Chief at one of Madison Avenue's tonier houses. About five-thirty on a Saturday afternoon, late in March, our doorman pushed the *revolving* door open for an arriving guest. Handing an expensive cowhide suitcase to a bellboy, the doorman caught my eye, gave me the high sign.

As I crossed the lobby I passed close to the incoming guest; he looked like a prosperous executive in his late thirties. Very well dressed, rather good-looking in a dark and serious fashion. He was carrying a pigskin brief case. I was sure I'd never seen him before.

The guest followed the bellboy to the registration desk.

The doorman said to me, "You wanted to know when they come outa the Vault, Mister Collans."

The "Vault" was lobby talk for a terminal checkroom. Sometimes a man who lives in town will deposit a suitcase in the Vault so he can withdraw it when he needs luggage for checking into a hotel with a girl. Naturally, in such cases the girl won't be his wife. "Taxi driver tell you?" I asked.

"No sir. I see that little yellow X on the end of the bag when I haul it outa the cab."

Attendants at Grand Central checkrooms sometimes make an inconspicuous cross with yellow crayon on the end of luggage which they know won't be called for within a day or so. The rack man can then save himself some lifting by stowing the marked bag on a rear shelf, leaving room up front for luggage which will move in and out every few hours.

"He don't even notice the mark, Mister Collans."

I went back of the Registration Desk. The clerk was handing a key to the bellboy who now had the brief case under his arm and was asking: "Are you expecting any mail or telegrams, Mister Murfrey?"

The guest shook his head.

When the bellboy had taken him up in the elevator I read the registration: *Harold A. Murfrey, Huntington, West Virginia.* He'd been given a single with shower, a seven-fifty room.

I asked the room clerk why he'd assigned a single to the Ninth. We had quite a few empties on lower floors; unless a guest says he particularly wants a room high up, we generally fill the lower floors first.

"He asked to be put on the ninth, Mister Collans."

"Say why?"

"Just said he liked to be on the ninth, that's all."

At that point it seemed likely Mister Murfrey might be planning to slip some cutie into his room without our knowing about it, so I put him on the Watch list right away. The phone board was notified, so were the maids on the ninth, the floor patrols, room service waiters and so on down the line.

When Charlie, the bellboy, came down I was at the captain's desk waiting for him. I watched while he wrote in the bell ledger:

UP	DOWN	ROOM	BAGS
5:40 P.M.	5:45 P.M.	935	2

I said: "What do y'know, Charlie?"

He knew I wasn't just making conversation. "Looked okay to me. But he's the large economy size, I'll say that. Offers you two-bits as if it was real money."

Being frugal about tipping isn't exactly a matter for the Security Chief to be concerned about. "Get a look at his belongings?"

"Yeah. He wanted a suit pressed. I rang the valet for him. Was there anything special you wanted me to look out for?"

"Just checking." I went down to the tailor shop.

The valet had just brought the suit down. A gray pin-striped worsted. Ready-made, good material, well worn. Bought at a 45th Street store. In New York, not West Virginia. No name on the pocket label.

The valet pointed out some faint brownish discolorations at the trouser's knees; he said they were nap scorches, made with a flatiron. Tailors use steam-heated pressing pads that leave a different kind of mark if *they* scorch. All it added up to was Murfrey was a man who pressed his own pants or else he had someone at home who pressed them for him. Probably a wife.

Nothing else turned up about Murfrey that night. Sunday morning about eleven the Security Office had a call from the Housekeeper to the effect that 935 seemed to be a sleepout. I went right up.

The floormaid who'd phoned the report to the House-keeper's office was still in Murfrey's room. She demonstrated that, though the bedclothes had been thrown back in disorder, as if the occupant had jumped out hastily, the bed hadn't been slept in at all. When a bed has been used, the wrinkles in the lower sheet get flattened by pressure; a maid who makes up fifteen rooms a day gets to notice things like that. There were wrinkles in Murfrey's sheets, but they were softly rounded, no flattened edges.

"Besides, Mister Collans," she pointed out, "he doesn't seem to have any pajamas or night clothes."

I looked in the closet and in his bag; she was right. Then I remembered the brief case Murfrey'd been carrying. It would have held a pair of pajamas, a toothbrush and razor, possibly a pair of slippers . . . and it wasn't there.

While the maid watched me, I fine-toothed that bag. All I came up with was the fact that two of his four-in-hands had been bought in a store in New Rochelle, New York and that none of the stuff in his bag looked flashy enough to be the wearables of a professional thief. But because of the man's request to be roomed on the ninth floor, I began to think Murfrey might be putting something over besides a bit of philandering.

A query to the phone switchboard netted me nothing; there hadn't been any calls to or from 935. I put a corridor patrol on the ninth floor, had him dressed in coveralls, tinkering with the fire hose.

Then I went down to the room-service pantry and talked to the Captain in charge. What I wanted to find out was whether someone on the eighth or ninth floor had been running up an unusually large total of charges in the week past.

The Captain consulted with his tray inspectors. (Any order served in a guest's room, even if it's a double planked sirloin with trimmings, is called a "tray.") They remembered two guests on those floors as having ordered unusually large amounts of food and drink. Especially drink.

One was a Greek importer; I dismissed him as a possible co-conspirator of Murfrey's. The Greek had been in the house nearly a month; he was well supplied with cash, according to the grapevine.

The other was a Mrs. Stehlti in 968.

"That dame, she's really a gourmet, Mister Collans! Look!" He dived into a file of phoned-in orders, came up with a slip. "For breakfast this morning, she orders a orange juice, *Peche* Irroy, shad roe and bacon with fresh asparagus and a side order scramble eggs, *croissants* and two pots coffee. An' a brandy to go with the coffee. Yeah, and a couple packs Parliaments."

It came to a little over eleven dollars; whole peaches in champagne aren't listed at cafeteria prices in that hotel. I rang the Rack, asked what they had on Mrs. Stehlti. What they had was a bill for $246, as I remember it. She'd come in one week before. There was no Previous Guest History on her. She hailed from Natchez, Mississippi, so her registration said.

The Cashier's office hadn't cashed any checks for her, or been asked to.

When I inquired about phone charges, there weren't any.

That decided me. Any out-of-towner who holes up in a metropolitan hotel for a solid week and doesn't use the phone is a suspicious character on my form sheet.

So I rounded up an Assistant Manager; we went up to 968, listened. The radio was on but we couldn't hear any voices.

I knocked. She opened the door right away. An extremely pretty brunette with a nice figure; I'd say she'd have been around twenty-five. She was smartly dressed; she really looked like the kind of girl who can afford a couple of hundred dollars worth of room-service a week.

She put on a good act, too. Surprised to see us but not embarrassed or alarmed when I told her I was the Chief House Officer. She laughed agreeably across the room-service table, supposed we'd come about her bill. Well, she was waiting for money to be wired from Natchez, expected it by that afternoon, would settle up right away.

She waited for us to apologize and leave. We didn't leave; there was no sign of any suitcases or bags. No hairbrushes or clothing or shoes or anything. And *her* bed, well, that had really been slept in! There wasn't anyone in her room then, though. If Murfrey'd been there overnight, he'd left. I looked in the closet and the bathroom.

I asked her if she meant to check out.

She said "Not at all; I expect to stay at least another week."

Then what, I inquired, had happened to her luggage?

Mrs. Stehlti laughed. She'd taken her bag to a friend's out on Long Island; had stupidly come back without it.

Of course she was lying. She couldn't have taken a suitcase out of the hotel without being questioned. But I pretended to fall for it.

I told her that, as the officer responsible for making sure guests who owed bills didn't remove their belongings, she'd get me in very wrong with the front office unless she called up her friend on Long Island right away and had her bags returned to the hotel without delay.

She became indignant then. Said I was insulting, doubting her word. She *wouldn't* call up her friend; if the hotel didn't trust her it knew what it could do!

What I did was leave the Assistant Manager there to

keep an eye on her, went down the corridor toward 935. As I passed my patrol, he said: "About five minutes ago he was talking to someone on the phone; I couldn't hear what he was saying."

A bellboy hurried down the corridor. I put a finger to my lips; he looked surprised but knocked on the 935 door without saying a word.

"Murfrey" opened the door. He tried to slam it shut soon as he saw me and the patrol officer but I had my foot in the door. "You called for a bellman, didn't you?" I pushed in.

"Yes, I did. But who're you?" He was rattled.

I told him, while I opened the second suitcase. It was locked; and there are rules about opening a guest's locked luggage but I didn't think he'd set up a holler. So I used the set of small skeletons that open any luggage lock except one of those keyless combination devices.

Mrs. Stehlti's suitcase was jam-crammed full of feminine things. I asked him if it was his bag.

He said it belonged to a friend.

I told him we had Mrs. Stehlti under guard. Were going to have them both arrested for a Switchover Swindle.

He did the only thing he could do. Offered to pay up for both of them if we'd forget the whole business.

I let him sweat awhile before I took him up on it. He and I went down to the Credit Manager's office where he spent another bad ten minutes convincing our credit man that his check for the $250 or so would be good. You see, the check he gave us wasn't signed Murfrey. It was another name beginning with M——; he had a wallet full of identification about himself under that name, including a number of membership cards in prominent New Rochelle clubs. Mixed in with his sales talk as to his check was a little stuff about wife trouble, short of funds, being under obligation to Mrs. Stehlti, so on.

We let him go and, after a session with Mrs. Stehlti, getting her signed admission of intent to defraud, we released her, too.

The Switchover is generally attempted by two men, however. Very seldom is it put on by a man *and* a woman, as in this case. Ordinarily, Crook A checks in with luggage, uses the room a week, meanwhile eating almost entirely off the hotel, either in the dining room or having meals served in the room. Generally there are a good many bar charges against the room, too. Sometimes Crook A will buy all the meals for Crook B during the week. In one instance the food and liquor charges ran well over the $300 mark before the Switch was pulled.

At the end of the week Crook B checks into another room with *his* luggage. He'll try to get on the same floor as Crook A, as near to his partner's room as possible. Crook B will charge no food or liquor; his bill will amount to little more than the actual tariff for the room.

Sometime that night, Crook A will pack his belongings, sneak his bag into B's room and leave it. Around noon the next day, when the bell staff is rushed, Crook B will call down to ask for a boy to take his bags; he's checking out. Chances are the bellboy who shows up won't be the one who roomed him. B was careful to check in after four o'clock, when the night-side goes on duty, now the day-side staff will be on the job.

Even if it should turn out to be the same one, the bellman would probably not remember that when B checked in he only had one suitcase, whereas he is now leaving with two. If it's a different bellman, of course there's no reason for him to suspect anything wrong. B goes to the cashier's desk, pays his one-night bill and leaves . . .

with A's luggage as well as his own. Outside the hotel he rejoins A.

Switchovers have been worked simultaneously in two hotels, with B checking in early in the week at the second house and A coming in to rescue him from the big bill there, at the end of the week. In this fashion two people can, theoretically, live pretty high on seven or eight dollars a week until they're caught. Catch is, a conviction on a Switchover indictment will be for conspiracy to defraud, meaning that the parties involved will not be living quite so high for about six or seven years. Since there's little chance of getting any real cash out of this particular swindle, it isn't as attractive as it might sound, to the guy with real larceny in his heart.

In putting a stop to the Murfrey version of the Switchover, I'd had help from our doorman, the desk clerk, the phone operators, a bellboy, a floormaid, a room-service captain and the cashier's office. That's what I meant when I said that teamwork is a lot more important in hotel security than the best guesswork.

But there have been times when I didn't have that teamwork, at least not until I'd pulled a head coach's locker-room pep talk on the staff. One of those times had to do with the Ninety-Nine Bottles that should have been hanging on the wall . . . and weren't.

XI

Ninety-Nine Bottles

ONE OF THE FRAMED photographs which hung in my various offices used to cause a good deal of curious comment. It showed a group of seventeen men and five women, the latter in black uniform dresses with white aprons and lace collars, the men in waiters' mess jackets or starched uniforms with tall chef's caps or open-collared work shirts. Only twenty of the twenty-two had faces in the picture. The features of the other two had been cut out so nothing but an oval of blank paper showed above their necklines.

I can recall those two missing faces much better than those of the others which remained to stare down over my shoulder, day after day.

The twenty-two were the permanent staff of the roof garden restaurant at a hotel where for some years I was Security Chief. The photograph was presented to me, mutilated, as a memento of my part in the affair of the vanishing champagne. An odd chain of circumstances accidentally brought to light a shortage of something like a hundred quarts of *Cordon Rouge,* worth in wine-list prices at that time around $900. Our front office became alarmed someone might have worked out a scheme for systematically looting the hotel's wine cellar. I was told to get to the bottom of the business *pronto.*

Checking up on other employees is the most disagreeable job a House Officer has to handle. Even if the morale of the staff is high, it isn't easy to question fellow workers about possible dishonesty.

A house detective engaged in protecting guests from room-riflers or bag-snatchers can always count on help from other employees. Even in cases where it's simply a problem of preventing a guest from putting over something on the hotel, a Security man can usually get cooperation. But the minute he begins to investigate the staff itself, he runs up against the old prejudice about informers.

Nobody likes to be called a squealer, whether the squeal is to a cop or a boss. And when employees feel as if the boss hasn't been giving them fair treatment, you haven't a Chinaman's chance of getting them to tell you if another worker is putting something over.

The employees in that hotel had what they considered was a real beef against the management. It had to do with the so-called "spotter system" of keeping tabs on personnel. Someone high-up in the Board of Directors had decided not to depend on the executive staff's judgment of how the hotel was being run but instead to hire one of the labor-spy agencies which make reports every month.

At intervals this agency would send around one of its snoopers, who'd check in as a guest and proceed to stir up more kinds of trouble than you'd think possible. Naturally, if he sent in reports stating that the hotel was well-run, excellently staffed with honest and courteous employees, pretty soon the agency would have had its contract canceled; there'd have been no point checking up on near perfection. So the reports had to show things were bad.

The snooper would proceed to demonstrate. He'd drop coins on the carpet where they wouldn't be conspicuous, hoping the floormaid would pick them up and pocket them. He'd leave a dollar bill in a suit sent to the valet, and if it was missing when the suit came back, the snooper would have a field day in his report.

He'd bait the phone operators at rush hours by asking them questions no busy phone girl could be expected to answer, and mark them down for discourtesy if they showed any irritation. He'd ask the bellman about that "good-looking blonde" down the corridor, hoping the bellman, in his eagerness to get a good tip, would break the inflexible rule about giving out any information about guests.

He'd rip a button off a shirt which he'd send to the laundry, and be real pleased if someone down in the laundry room forgot to sew it on before the shirt was sent back.

To get something on an employee, there wasn't a trick in the book those snoopers wouldn't try from leaving a half-full bottle of liquor on the bureau in hopes some maid or room-service waiter would snitch a nip, to dropping a wallet under the table in the dining room where a busboy would be sure to pick it up and perhaps forget to return it.

On the snooper's Daily Report sheet there were blanks for notations on Politeness, Promptness, Neatness, Salesmanship and so on, but the space reserved for Comments was where the snooper really went to town. After two or three days of goading an elevator man into telling him where he could "get down a little bet on a good thing at Belmont," or inducing a friendly barman to tip him off to where he might "pick up a little company for the evening," the snooper'd generally be able to send in quite a batch of juicy reports.

Members of the hotel unions were bitter about such *agents provocateur;* the unions were fighting for contracts which made it tough for hotels to fire employees except for downright discourtesy or dishonesty. A lot of the hotel people felt one of the main reasons the management paid for such snooping was to be able to frame any individual they wanted to get rid of.

Truth was, the Front Office, and certainly the Security Office, hated that spy system. It made bad feeling all through the hotel. The staff was always on the lookout for spotters. Minute one was identified as such, the word went up and down the grapevine. Once in a while an innocent guest would be suspected of being a spotter, then he'd wonder why he got such scornful glances and surly service.

You build up an attitude like that among the help, and if they get wind of anybody cheating the hotel or stealing from it, they're likely to grin behind their hands and say nothing. That was about the situation we had when the champagne began to disappear.

My security staff of eight was supposed to keep a watchful eye on all of the hotel's fifteen hundred regular employees. But in addition there were hundreds of people working in the house who weren't on the permanent pay roll. Some of these were hired by the lessees of various concessions, theater tickets, florists, gift shop, washroom, public stenographer, barbershop and so on. We had no control over these people at all, yet we were supposed to see they didn't put anything over.

The bulk of the nonpermanent help, however, were waiters, barmen, bus-girls and dishwashers called in from time to time to supplement the regular staff. Most of these extras were hired on the occasion of big social affairs, charity balls, debutante parties. In the ordinary course of events no one on the Security Staff would even see most of these extras.

The first suspicion we had that champagne was doing a

113

disappearing act came during a coming-out party for one of those synthetic glamour debs. A real snooty event, covers for a thousand in the Moonbeam Roof, orchids and Cartier keepsakes, big-name bands, acts from the hit revues, dancing-until-breakfast . . . the works.

You'd have thought expense was of no importance to the parents of the well-publicized young lady. But though there'd been no argument about prices when the affair'd been arranged with our Banquet Manager, a few days after the party the girl's mother became cost-conscious. Maybe she'd been burned up about certain cracks in the gossipapers referring to million-heiresses who fancied they could buy their way into the Charmed Circle and would presently find out it couldn't be done.

Anyhow, mother criticized several items on the bill sent along by the Banquet Department. One was a charge for fifty cases of Mumms *Cordon Rouge*. Now, fifty cases is six hundred quarts, each of which should fill six to seven of those hollow-stemmed, saucer-brimmed champagne glasses. Say four thousand servings, in round numbers, which would have worked out to four glasses for each guest.

A fair average for shindigs of this sort is two glassfuls per cover. Some at the tables won't drink at all; many will stop at one glass, thereafter switching to other stimulants. Once in a while a dinner exclusively for young people will show a three-serving average; not often. So either a lot of the revelers had been feeling no pain when they left the Moonbeam Roof or the deb's parents had been overcharged.

Evidently mother hadn't figured all that out; she merely felt the round number'd been dreamed up to raise the ante on her. Her complaint—and it wasn't unreasonable—was that her guests *couldn't* have put away exactly fifty cases. Possibly forty-two and a half, or some odd number. The figure of fifty sounded too pat.

It was, too. The chances were a million to one against a round fifty cases, particularly since there'd been no stinting on the supply. Yet the Banquet Department records showed that quantity *had* been checked out of our wine cellar. None had been returned, though considerable amounts of Scotch, Bourbon, Irish, cordials and cognacs had been left over, sent back downstairs.

The fact no champagne had been left over was enough to make me suspicious. After a blowout like that, a few of the departing guests might have taken along a half-empty bottle of bubbly when they left their scrambled eggs and sausages at 7 A.M. But if as much as a case should have been carried away in that fashion, it would have been unusual. So the first question was, how had the leftover champagne left the hotel?

None of the Roof's permanent staff could, or would, give me any helpful suggestions. The head barman passed the buck to the extra waiters who'd been hired for the occasion; if there'd been any finagling, he was sure the "temporaries" must have engineered it.

The Roof's headwaiter, who was responsible for hiring the outside help, was equally certain none of his extras had been mixed up in anything so dishonest as wholesale liquor theft. I questioned every one of the twenty-two . . . and got nowhere.

The Banquet Manager made a diplomatic adjustment in the bill to the deb's mamma. The Front Office began to build up a head of steam. If somebody, or several somebodies, had worked out a way to sneak nearly a thousand bucks worth of wine out of the hotel in a single evening, no telling how large the losses might be if the scheme wasn't scotched quickly. Pantry raiding on a grand scale could be serious, with a quarter of a million dollars worth of drinkables under our *Sommelier's* lock and key.

The Resident Manager put it right in the lap of the Security Office. And, at the same time, without notifying me, made arrangements with the agency supplying the snoopers to put one of their men on the job. What the agency did was simply to go to one of the union waiters who hired out as an extra and pay him a bonus to spy on his fellows.

I didn't learn about that until a few nights later when there was a big organization Anniversary Ball in the Moonbeam Roof. Meantime I'd made some arrangements of my own. I fixed it so all the empty bottles coming down from the Roof would go to the wine cellar, where the bottle-buster would make a count of the champagne empties. Liquor bottles have to be smashed to prevent their being sold by junkmen to unscrupulous parties who might refill them with cut stuff.

Also, I arranged for one of my corridor patrols to act as operator on the service elevator which ran to the Roof. During the evening I made a couple of trips through the Roof kitchens and bar, watching for any place where quart bottles might be hidden temporarily. I discovered nothing except that the toastwoman had caught on to the fact that one of the extra waiters was a snooper. She took some pains to bawl him out, while I was in earshot, for hanging around in the kitchen when he should have been out looking after his table. Probably she hadn't been the first to spot him as a snooper, but she plainly wanted to tip me off about him.

The word had been passed down the line, evidently *via* the Banquet Manager's office, that if any more wines or liquors went AWOL, up on the Roof, the entire permanent staff would be looking for new jobs. I think some of them had the idea that if the snooper found out how the champagne had been stolen, his report would make it seem as if they'd all been implicated and they'd be fired anyhow. That's the only way I can account for what happened.

The Anniversary party began to break up about two-thirty in the morning. By three o'clock I had the head barman's report on liquors used; the totals withdrawn from the wine cellar less those ready for return. Twenty minutes later I had the check figures on empties taken downstairs. They didn't add up.

Thirty-five cases of *Blondel-Marchal* had been ordered up, four hundred twenty quarts. But this had been a dinner for people who were somewhat older than the champagne-thirsty younger set at the debutante affair; more of the men preferred whiskies. Twenty-eight of the four hundred twenty quarts had been returned to the wine cellar unopened. So there should have been three hundred ninety-two empty *Blondel-Marchal* bottles. The bottle buster reported only two hundred ninety-three. Somehow ninety-nine bottles were missing.

The figures on whiskey and cognac withdrawals tallied with the downstairs totals of empties and returns. Only the champagne had disappeared.

The headwaiter, the head barman and I made an immediate search of the Roof. We poked into every possible corner where a dozen bottles could have been concealed. We found nothing.

The part-time waiters, bus-girls and dishwashers had gone off duty by the time our search party had finished. My Security man on the service car was positive none of the temporary help had gotten away with anything larger than a bottle of Tabasco. The only good thing about his report was that the snooper-waiter had left before anyone was sure there'd been a repetition of the theft. He wouldn't be able to throw much light on the matter.

We lined up the rest of the permanent staff and put it up to them: some of them *must* know who was getting away with the champagne. None of them would admit to knowing a thing, though I got the feeling one of the coffee men might have done some talking if I'd had him down in my office with none of the others around.

We went down to the Banquet Manager's office, the headwaiter and I, sat there and considered the various possibilities for perhaps an hour. It must have been close to five when we gave it up as a bad job.

When I got back to my office and switched on the light, the first thing I saw was a bunch of celery tops arranged in a water tumbler as if they were jonquils. So I couldn't possibly have overlooked it, this vegetable bouquet had been planted in the middle of my desk blotter.

Someone had taken a good deal of trouble and a certain amount of risk in putting that frazzled bunch of chewed-up stalks in my office. It was too clearly a hint to be disregarded. I took the celery tops to the service car, went down to the basement to put them where they belonged, in the garbage cans.

I was just in time. The twenty-odd containers stood along the curb by the delivery entrance. A quick inspection showed me that the four nearest the platform must be those which had been sent down from the Moonbeam Roof. I'd just dug down into the first of them and recovered a full bottle with the gold and black collar and the buff label, when the Sanitation Department truck pulled up.

There were two city employees in gray denim aboard; they tried not to seem surprised at seeing me. But they were uneasy as they started to hoist up the heavy cans and dump them into the truck. Actually I didn't have a thing on those two. I had to put up a bluff, telling them their only chance was to play along with me unless they wanted me to take their badge numbers, report them to their superintendent.

For a few minutes they pretended not to know what I was driving at, but when I told them not to dump the last four cans and showed them the bottle of *Blondel-Marchal,* they decided to take their chances with me rather than with their boss.

They let me ride on the truck. The setup, they told me, was for them to meet a small pick-up truck half a dozen blocks from the hotel and turn over the champagne which by that time would be sacked in burlap bags. All they were supposed to get out of it was twenty bucks apiece, every night they were told to watch out for the bottles.

The pick-up truck was waiting. The driver was the Roof's vegetable cook; the man waiting on the sidewalk ready to grab the burlap bags was the head barman. They came back to the hotel with me after a little scuffle.

The barman's brother worked in a 52nd Street night club; they had turned over the wine stolen from the deb's party to him and were to split the proceeds. We got witnessed confessions and a promise to return something like ten cases of *Cordon Rouge* which the vegetable cook had packed into five garbage cans on the evening of the coming-out party. Then I made them go down with me and unload the four cans of pea pods, olive pits, celery tops, potato peelings and plate scrapings which had been tamped down over the ninety-nine missing bottles of *Blondel-Marchal.*

There wasn't any prosecution. We notified the union

that neither of the two culprits should be allowed to work in hotels or restaurants again, at least not where they'd be able to indulge in that kind of champagne binge.

So the garbage-can pipeline got no publicity; aside from the Front Office the only people who knew what had happened were the other twenty employees on the Roof permanent staff. At least one of them, of course, knew about it before being told officially by their head-waiter, but I never found out which it was. Possibly the coffee man; he'd have been making trips to the refuse cans to dump coffee grounds and may have seen a bottle-neck under its garland of pea pods.

Probably all he'd meant to do was give me a lead to the stolen wine without getting involved as a squealer. He managed to accomplish more than that. Within a month the higher-ups had a change of heart about the snooper system. Apparently they were ready to agree that if the Security Office could handle a matter like the disappearing champagne so much better than the outside agency, it ought to be able to keep an eye on such lesser items as employee honesty and courtesy. Anyway, their contract was canceled.

There was no mention of that when the Roof staff sent me the framed photograph which had been taken a few months before the events I've just told about. All that was on the picture was four lines neatly written across the white aprons of the ice-cream chef and the buffet man:

> *Ninety-nine bottles a-hangin' on the wall*
> *If one of them bottles should happen to fall*
> *There'd be ol' Dev Collans*
> *With his eye on the ball*

XII

The Lady Is a Stooge

I NEVER SPENT much time on crossword puzzles; any time I felt my brain cells needing baffling, there was always the Lost & Found Department. Some of the things guests, departing, left behind them were real riddles.

Lingerie, toilet articles, pajamas, slippers, rubbers, umbrellas and hats were turned in by floormaids at the rate of one every hour around the clock. Those were simple cases of forgetfulness. But why did the guest from Greenwich, Conn. leave a brass saluting cannon, complete with blanks? Had he been hoping to startle, from his tenth floor window, some convivial acquaintance down on the avenue? Some lady descending from her metered chariot? We never knew.

Girdles, corsets, braces, spectacles, false teeth, false eyes, false hair and even false bosoms. (I sometimes wondered about the circumstances in *such* instances!) came to our L & F in routine quantities. But what miracle came to pass to cause one elderly gentleman from Detroit to leave a pair of perfectly good rubber-tipped crutches? Was the food in our establishment so superior, the air of our upper floors so tonic, that after a four-day stay the old boy took a new lease on life? Or had some more stimulating influence been at work, there?

Tiny turtles with initials painted on their backs, glass bowls of guppies or goldfish, an elaborate but empty canary cage (there might have been a minor tragedy in that one) all turned up at the room next my Security Office "to be held until called for."

I suppose the difficulty of taking such pets home accounted for some of those livestock items. But what lay behind the abandonment of the twenty-foot rope ladder which was turned in from the twelfth-floor room of a young man registered from Honolulu? We speculated on his having had notions of attempting a human-fly descent to a room on the eleventh for purposes of theft or romance. But the room beneath his had been vacant, so if he'd tried such a stunt, he must have been a considerably disappointed daredevil.

If you've traveled to any extent, the chances are you have, at some time, left some possession behind in your hotel room. If it was worth the trouble, you probably wrote asking if it had been found and would the hotel be so good as to return it? In which case you'd have received a polite form letter containing the line: *We are glad to advise you that the property has been found and is being sent to address given.*

You may have wondered why they didn't notify you "at address given" as soon as the article *was* found, which would have been within an hour of your check-out. The case of Mr. S—— may explain.

It—and others like it—were the reasons for hotels dropping the practice of sending on to a guest any articles left in his room.

Mr. S—— was a distiller from P——, Illinois. One Friday in November, Mr. and Mrs. S—— checked in for a week end, picking up a reservation made a week earlier for a parlor-bedroom suite. They were a good-looking, very well-dressed couple. Also, they were the kind of guests a hotel likes, they ate in our dining room most of the time, ordered the best liquors from room-service, tipped liberally.

So when it was discovered, after they'd checked out, that Mrs. S—— had left behind a pair of crimson, ostrich-feathered-trimmed mules, the L & F Department hastened to return the obviously-overlooked property to its desirable patrons. The mules were nicely packaged, mailed back to Mr. S—— at P——.

We heard the repercussions all the way from Illinois. The lady who'd registered with Mr. S——, it seemed, hadn't been his wife . . . but a local charmer well known to the real Mrs. S——. So well known, in fact, that when the package was delivered to the S—— home, not to the gentleman's office, Mrs. S—— immediately recognized the feathered mules.

There was no way for Mr. S—— to lie out of it. He couldn't save face . . . and trouble . . . by claiming the hotel had made a mistake in returning someone else's property to him. Those mules were the red flag to an enraged Mrs. S——. She sued for divorce and alienation of affections; she named the co-respondent in no affectionate terms. As a result several of our employees were handed subpoenas for testifying at the trial.

It did happen, in that particular case, that the ending wasn't as bad as the beginning. The divorce was granted. As I remember it, the alimony allowed was on the astronomical order. But the lady of the crimson mules, in course of time, became the rightful Mrs. S——. She and her now-lawful husband returned to New York, spent part of their honeymoon in the same room in which the slippers had been discovered. Possibly an anticlimax from a romantic point of view, still a nice touch of sentiment which could be appreciated by a House Officer.

The reason Lost & Found articles were taken in charge by the Chief House Officer was that so often items reported stolen were later Found to have been merely Lost. Never did more than three or four days go by without some woman guest letting out a loud squawk about having been "robbed."

She would just *know* the maid had latched onto the platinum wristwatch, or the topaz bracelet, or whatever. She could tell by the "sneaky expression" on that maid's face she wasn't to be trusted, and so forth . . . and on and on.

While I'd be down on hands and knees searching those old, familiar places where forgetful females always seem to hide their valuables, I'd remind the complaining lady that our maids regularly turned in better than a thousand dollars each month, bills and coins found in guests' rooms after check-outs. So it seemed unlikely one of those same maids would appropriate a guest's jewelry, when she'd already passed up large sums of ready cash.

The argument was seldom convincing. Any woman sufficiently suspicious of her fellow human beings to *cache* her valuables in some ridiculous hiding place, and forgetful enough not to remember what she'd done with them, would naturally be hard to reason with.

So I'd have to point out the notices, framed under glass in every room, emphasizing that the hotel accepted no liability in the case of valuables lost from rooms when they might have been put in the cashier's safe downstairs.

Meanwhile I'd be looking in the customary hidy-holes where, experience taught me, women were apt to conceal stuff, and then draw a blank on the matter. Beneath sofa or chair cushions. Under mattresses and inside them. (I've known women to snip open a mattress ticking with manicure scissors, to create a homemade safe deposit vault). Inside pillow slips. Under lamp bases. Beneath the edge of carpeting. Tucked in the drapery tie-backs. Stuck on top of wooden valances. Stuck, by means of Mr. Wrigley's product, underneath bureau drawers. No Customs Inspector could have given *me* lessons in cockeyed hiding places.

If the maids were suspected of taking money, I looked first between the pages of the Gideon Bible or the yellow pages in the Classified phone directory. Sometimes a bill would merely have been laid between sheets of notepaper in the writing desk drawer. Once I found a twenty crammed into the socket of a bureau light fixture which didn't seem to be working when I switched it on. The dear lady'd rammed it down into the socket, screwed the light bulb down on top of it!

Should the "stolen" bauble be a pin, I fine-toothed the draperies, shower curtains, all hanging garments. Once I unearthed a bar-pin inside the lining of a grandmotherly woman's hat. The owner simply couldn't *believe* she'd put it there; she thought she must have been so concerned about the pin's safety she'd gotten up in her sleep and "put it where no one'd be likely to take it."

Rings mysteriously found their way to the narrow tops of door mouldings, beneath ink wells in the little socket of the writing desk drawer, on window ledges outside the window! Checking these possibilities took time but were simple compared to the problem of locating a "stolen" item which the owner had concealed in her own luggage. Getting a complainant to really search her own baggage was sometimes difficult.

When it got to the point where I was convinced the allegedly stolen article wasn't in the guest's room, that either she'd hidden it on her person or, more likely, hadn't brought it along to begin with, I simply suggested calling in the police. Often this would tone the lady down. Sometimes the shock of being faced with the necessity of making a formal accusation would make the guest recall where she'd really put the precious item.

Occasionally we had other claims of robbery which we suspected were phony but could never quite prove. These excited alarms always concerned extremely valuable gems; invariably the victim would be someone who wouldn't mind getting his, or her, name in large, black type on the front pages.

The trouble with that sort of publicity-theft was, if the actress or singer or dancer got her headlines, the hotel would get a black eye for supposedly allowing jewel thieves to run wild in its corridors.

The same held true for another class of phonies—the stooges in framed-up divorce cases. If the principals were of enough importance, when the case came to court there'd be a juicy smear of references to "adulterous cohabitation" and often the hotel would be made to appear as if its employees had been winking at this sort of shenanigans right along.

Here is an actual report in which the hotel *was* named, though I won't include it here. It was headed DESCRIBE HOTEL RENDEZVOUS:

It was quite a party that gathered at 10:30 p.m. last May 26 outside D—— W——'s room on the eighth floor of the Hotel Z——. There was Mrs. H—— Y—— a tall, attractive young woman; her brothers T—— and R—— A——; private detective R—— M—— and two assistants. They rapped on the door and after a discreet interval were admitted by Miss ———, a small, shapely blonde, Mr. M—— testified in Supreme Court today. They "trouped into the room and found Mrs. Y——'s husband, J—— Y——. Miss W. was wearing a yellow negligee and slippers," Mr. M—— testified. "Y—— had on shorts and stockings. There was a single bed in the room and the covering was mussed."

The detective was the first witness in Mrs. Y——'s suit for a divorce from J—— Y——.

I have no way of knowing whether this particular "raid" was a frame-up but it bore all the earmarks. The damage to the hotel lay in the fact that if it *was* a case of collusion, the newspaper's readers wouldn't know it. In their minds, Hotel Z—— would be marked as a "riding academy," a place where any couple possessed of the price and the inclination could latch up without benefit of clergy.

Behind the scenes of these staged raids are the lawyers for the parties who "have agreed to disagree." According to the laws of some states, at least, the couple who've decided to call it quits mustn't settle things in an amicable way but instead must get nasty about it. Usually the lawyers hire some private detective agency to arrange the casting for these bedroom farces.

The private investigator employs some model, actress or perhaps his own secretary, to act as the adulterous female. He arranges it so she and the husband will check in at the hotel, notifies the wife's attorney when the raid should be timed . . . and the lecherous couple, who have usually been eyeing each other dismally and confining their intimate remarks to the Dodgers' chances or the Rangers' scoring, will be "surprised" apparently in *flagrante delicto,* as the legal bigwigs nice-nelly it.

House Officers hate this sort of setup because it makes them out to be dumb at their jobs. No house detective wants to get mixed up in a case where, should he be called for testimony, it would have to be to the effect that he'd been negligent in spotting a couple illegally enjoying bedded bliss while the private detective has been smart enough to trail them and nail them in the act.

Also, most House Officers have a low opinion of private operatives from small agencies. A sizable percentage of all hotel detectives are graduates, if that's the right word, of the larger Investigating Bureaus.* Pinkertons, Burns, Valentines and others of equivalent size or standing have in years past been the training grounds for many top Security men.

Police detectives occasionally get into the work after retirement but few of them are temperamentally suited to the job. Any member of the Force gets, willy-nilly, into the habit of telling people where to head in and when to move on. This doesn't fit in with the attitude required by hotel managements, which demand a little more suavity and savoir-faire than a precinct plain-clothes man is apt to acquire on his round of official duties.

Much as Security officers dislike *The Lady Is A Stooge* being staged as an amateur performance in one of the hotel's bedrooms, their resentment is much sharper toward methods used by private investigators where there *isn't* any collusion. I've known operatives to attach amplifying devices to the walls of adjoining rooms so a tape recording of amorous conversations between an erring wife and her current Casanova might be introduced into court records.

Attempts at bribing bellmen and room-service waiters to repeat to these divorce-dicks what was going on in

---

* The proportion gets smaller year by year; more and more Security men are recruited from the ranks of hotel employees, bellmen and elevator men, in particular, providing a steadily larger percentage of candidates.

Room So-and-So, were too numerous to catalog. On several occasions, female operatives—of small agencies specializing in such smelly business—put on uniforms resembling those used by our floormaids, obtained entrance into the room occupied by some unlawfully bedded couple.

One male operative lay in wait for a suspected couple and, with a flash-bulb camera, snapped a picture of the sinful pair as they emerged from their room in the morning. This Inquiring Photographer had his camera smashed and lost a new denture plate in the fracas which followed. But the wandering husband lost his case in court, too.

On only one occasion have I tangled violently with a man surprised in what the papers coyly refer to as a "clandestine relationship." I still bear the marks.

Shortly after dinnertime one March evening a couple of white-belted Shore Patrols were brought to my office by an Assistant Manager. They wanted my assistance in the matter of a guest, registered as Lieutenant Commander A. R. Josephson and Wife, in Room 1628. The Lieutenant Commander was suspected of being a phony; in fact it was certain he wasn't what he'd represented himself to be, since there was no Lt. Commander by that name on the Navy's roster. Moreover, the Shore Patrols had been tipped off that the young fellow was actually a Petty Officer named John Saldinn, long AWOL and down on the books, technically, as a deserter.

I remembered the Lieutenant Commander, youthfully grim-faced and serious, extremely attentive to his pretty brunette wife. His uniform had fitted handsomely; his bearing had been all a Naval Academy drillmaster would have desired. I hadn't looked for the amethyst ring which all Annapolis graduates wear but he'd certainly looked as if he'd been entitled to one.

Other bits of information came to light as I checked his Guest History card, his room bill, the bell ledger, his phone charges. The gentleman had never favored us with his presence before. He was evidently a liberal provider and a good spender; on the strength of his commission he'd cashed personal checks for nearly three hundred dollars. Although he'd been in the house some forty-eight hours, neither he nor the brunette had made any outside phone calls whatever. And on the bell-ledger was a record of delivery to his room of *Plane Tix*.

A query to the Transportation Desk brought forth the fact that Lt. Commander and Mrs. Josephson had seats aboard a Pan American flying boat bound for South America, the following morning. Few Navy men, as the Shore Patrols pointed out, have to resort to such a way of obtaining transportation anywhere overseas!

By the time I'd rounded up these suggestive facts, two ranking Naval Officers had arrived and were waiting down in the lobby. It was arranged that the Assistant Manager and I, with the Shore Patrols as support, should proceed to the sixteenth floor, wait outside the room. After giving us time to get there, one of the officers from the Naval District would call the Lieutenant Commander on the house phone, ask him to come down to the lobby.

If the man refused to answer his phone, we were to go in with master keys. If he decided to make a sudden dash to get out, the Shore Patrols would nab him—they said.

We went up. The phone rang in the room. We heard the brunette answer, saying that her husband wasn't in.

Since the elevator operator and one of the desk clerks had been sure the Lieutenant Commander *had* gone up to his room, we waited.

After some five minutes, I knocked on the door, intending to ask the girl if I might inspect the lighting fixtures or the radio receiver, as a stall to get in the room. Instantly the door opened in my face; he must have had his hand on the knob when I'd rapped. I *know* he had his fist on me before I could grab him. He chopped at me with the short stiff jab of the boxer. It felt as if he was wearing brass knuckles when the blow landed just above my right eyebrow.

There were a couple of exciting minutes, then the Patrols had him and the house doctor had me. It took three stitches to close the cut his ring had gashed in my forehead; it was just an ordinary onyx signet ring, not an amethyst.

The Assistant Manager had *his* hands full, too: the brunette simply would not believe her handsome husband of only a week was an impostor. She raged and screamed, arousing other guests. We couldn't put her out; she wouldn't *go* out, wouldn't get dressed, wouldn't do anything but howl to high heaven.

Not until one of the officers came up, put through a call to the genuine Mrs. Saldinn, let her talk to the brunette, did things quiet down on the sixteenth floor. And then the house doctor had to give the bereaved "bride" a shot in the arm to get her in shape to dress and leave.

Sometimes when I absent-mindedly put my fingers to my forehead and feel that small ridge of scar tissue, I think about the only other time I intervened in what might have been called a marital mixup. It was only a few years ago so perhaps it's too early to say for sure how the marriage is going to work out. But I was pretty pleased with my part in it.

One summer morning very early I had a call from one

of my floor patrols: woman in 1090 crying to beat the band.

It's SHOP* to keep close watch on female guests who have fits of weeping. I made a rapid reconnaissance of what facts I could find out about 1090. A Mr. and Mrs. Harold Greening, from Elizabeth City, North Carolina. Checked in the night before. No room service. Half a dozen local phone calls, no long distance.

Greening, of course, is one of those names which like Smithson or Johnson or Browning, are almost as frequently used for *noms des hotels* as John Doe is for subpoenas and indictments.

One of the bellmen remembered them: nice, quiet couple, might have been honeymooners, almost. Good luggage, two suitcases.

An elevator man thought a dark-haired young fellow, corresponding to the bellman's description of Mr. Greening, had gone out, alone, around midnight.

That was the sum of it when I went up to the Tenth to listen outside her room. She was still bawling her heart out . . . it didn't sound like a crying jag to me. I used the floor phone to call the night nurse up from the house hospital. When she got there I knocked on the door.

The sobbing stopped at once. A weepy voice inquired what I wanted. I had the nurse answer, asking if there was anything she could do to help Mrs. Greening.

If the young lady'd made some reply such as, "No, there's nothing anybody can do," or words to that effect, my worries would have increased. That's sometimes suicide talk.

But Mrs. Greening opened the door. She was in a negligee over a nightgown; she was real pretty even with no make-up and the red-rimmed eyes. She didn't seem too

* Standard Hotel Operating Procedure.

surprised when she saw me and managed a small smile for the nurse. Yes, there *was* something : could the nurse bring a sleeping pill? She wasn't, she said, used to taking the things so one would be enough.

I said our nurse would be glad to get one for her; if there was anything else she wanted all she had to do was lift the phone and ask. Mrs. Greening thanked me shyly. I left her in the nurse's hands, went back down to my office, made a notation on my Daily Activity Report:

Investigated guest crying in 1090. Asked night nurse for phenobarb pill. Nurse took over.

As it happened, I was the one who took over. Half an hour later the nurse stopped by my office. She perched on the corner of my desk in her crisp white uniform and asked if she might talk off the record for a minute?

I told her to go ahead; I'd keep whatever she had on her mind, to myself.

Well, she told me, this nice kid up in 1090 wasn't Mrs. Greening at all, she wasn't Mrs. Anybody. That was the trouble; she wanted terribly to be the wife of the young man with whom she'd registered as man and wife. Had been in love with him for a year now, had been sleeping with him every now and then, was sure the lad was in love with her, still no prospect of wedding bells or even a quick ceremony down at City Hall.

"Mrs. Greening" was, the nurse said, convinced the man never would marry. It wasn't a question of money; *he* was doing very nicely as night announcer on a local radio station and she herself was a secretary with a big paper corporation, making good money. The trouble was the young man's mother.

Mother, it seemed, had apron strings the size of tug hawsers. Didn't like Harold to go with *any* girl; if she'd known he'd been sleeping with Joan ("Mrs. Greening") it would just about kill her. In fact, she'd often told Harold that if he ever married, it would cause his mother's death.

The nurse had been sympathetic enough to get Joan's confidence; had learned "Greening's" real name.

"I think it's a rotten shame," she finished, "that some selfish old woman can keep a couple of nice kids like that apart, that is, assuming he *is* a nice youngster and not just a heel who's conning the girl along."

I told her there wasn't much use getting wrought up about it, since she couldn't do anything about it.

My friend in the white uniform rubbed her chin with the knuckle of a clenched fist. "I know what I'd do about it if I was a man," she had a challenging glint in her eye. "I'd go over and talk to that boy friend of Joan's; I'd throw the fear of God into him. One of these fine mornings that poor child is going to wake up and find herself pregnant. Then she's liable to take a dive out the window."

I reminded her that such a predicament couldn't be charged against the hotel management. That it was none of her business or of mine what happened in such an affair. That I was going just as far as I could, further than I should, by letting the girl stay after finding out she wasn't married to her roommate.

Then, after the nurse, sorely disappointed in me, I'm sure, had gone back to the hospital suite, I went over to Station WHEN, to give it call letters it never had. I didn't go as a representative of the hotel, I made that clear to Harold, who turned out to be a regular guy. Maybe I did go overboard a bit on telling him what a man ought to do in circumstances like that. And how he

134

could do it, if he wanted to, without his mother being any the wiser, for the time being.

He listened; he seemed impressed. But he didn't make any promises, didn't even try to suggest he might decide to do the right thing by Joan. He did say he understood how I felt and, of course, how Joan felt about it. He thanked me for my visit and shook hands politely.

I went away feeling like the small boy who slapped blackberry jam on his bee sting; it might not have done any good but it couldn't do much harm and it made me feel better for a minute, anyway.

It made Joan feel better, too. A week or so after that dawn patrol across town to the radio station I had a warm "Thank You" note on expensive notepaper with *Mrs. Harold Greening* across the top in imitation engraving. *"Thank you for giving me the nicest thing I've ever had in my life,"* it began.

Only the name printed there wasn't *Greening,* to be sure. She'd changed it to the right one.

XIII

Lizzies and Queens

AFTER SOME YEARS on the job I got so I could tell time by the complexion of the crowd in the lobby. If people were striding briskly to and from the elevators, with many more men than women in evidence, that would probably be in the morning, between eight and nine. A half-empty lobby, with more women than men in sight, mid-morning. A great bustle and commotion, with many in the throng obviously not guests, and groups of three or four men clustered together, lunchtime.

About five-thirty in the afternoon the pace would have slowed down and there'd be almost as many women as men milling around. Then the percentage of women would decline until, say, nine, when theatergoers had mostly drifted out. From nine to eleven-thirty we'd have to keep an eye on twice as many men as women. Then for an hour or so it would be nearly fifty-fifty. After half-past twelve the ratio would drop to one female to every four or five men.

But the proportion of "undesirables" was *at all times* double as many women as men. And many of these females weren't on the make for male companionship at all.

An "undesirable" might have been a shoplifter or a sob-story artist, a fur-trapper or a bag-snatcher; a lavatory-worker or a Lesbian in pursuit of her prey. Dealing with any of them was, always, to me the most disagreeable part of my job.

Perhaps you never heard of shoplifters in a hotel? Well, maybe that's the wrong term. Almost every one with whom I had to deal admitted tearfully she wasn't really a shoplifter,—she merely suffered from kleptomania. In spite of all she could do to control herself, she was under some mysterious compulsion to take things which didn't belong to her even when she didn't need them, or want them. I came to the conclusion this peculiar mania affected only rich women; those who aren't so well-heeled get to be called ordinary shoplifters.

I've caught 'em swiping flowers out of lobby vases; sometimes trying to get away with the vases, too. One old girl pinched three desk pads from our public writing desks on the mezzanine. When I had the maid give the guest's room a frisko, enough hotel stationery turned up to circularize the entire membership of the D.A.R. and underneath the envelopes was one of our registration desk pens the old girl had evidently taken right under the clerk's nose.

Some of these pilferers would snake decorative runners off end tables in the lobby, stuff 'em in their coats. One made a try at walking off with the big bronze candelabra which stood beneath a pier glass on a side table next the Hospitality Desk. Another, a plump, white-haired, grandmotherly party who was a "permanent" in one of the luxury suites had the habit of fooling around the newsstand for an hour every afternoon, waiting until the clerk's attention had been diverted; then would slip a two-bit magazine or a paper-back book under her coat, confident nobody'd noticed her. We finally gave up on her, simply added the amount of the purloined items to her laundry bill.

The sob-story artists were much more annoying pests. They were generally teen-agers who panhandled around the lobby or mezzanine. After picking out a likely sucker, the pitch might have been that the kid had expected to meet a friend or relatives at the hotel but the other girl hadn't shown up and the unhappy young lady was stranded with only a little change in her purse. Sometimes these youngsters would make a bid for "just enough to phone home." Occasionally they'd try for train or bus fare, if they figured the sucker would stand for that big a bite.

Ordinarily they'd start out by picking on motherly women of sympathetic appearance, but sooner or later they'd try to put the tap on some older man. We had to break up that sort of thing if we could, though often the sucker would bawl us out for being unfeeling in our attitude toward "this poor, homesick child." Sometimes those things developed into under-age seduction, with the man unaware he'd been fooling with "jail-bait."

The fur-trappers were older and bolder. They weren't playing for peanuts. I knew of one such lobby thief who admitted stealing between fifteen and twenty thousand dollars worth of furs from the midtown terminal hotels in New York in a single month.

They had a dozen ways of setting a trap for the unwary fur-bearing guest. Say a Miss Anne Graham, a well-to-do young lady, had made an appointment to meet a friend in our lobby late some afternoon. It would be cold outside but warm in the hotel; after a while Miss Graham would shuck her silver fox or toss her ranch mink over the arm of her chair.

Along would come a fur-trapper, also a personable young woman, who would appear to be looking for someone. She would stop beside Miss Graham's chair, inquire amiably if the young woman was Elsie Brown?

"No," the victim would say, "I'm Anne Graham."

The fur-trapper would apologize agreeably, saunter away, still apparently on the lookout for Elsie Brown.

A few minutes later a page boy would call out: "Miss Graham . . . ? Call for Miss Graham . . ."

The victim would stand up, waving. The page boy would hurry over, hold out a silver tray on which there'd be a slip: "PLEASE CALL Bryant 2-2222."

Miss Graham would ask directions to the nearest phone. The page boy would point; naturally Miss Graham's eyes would follow the boy's glance.

He'd pocket his tip, go away. She'd turn to pick up her coat. It wouldn't be there. Unless some House Officer had been on the spot, the silver fox or mink would be walking out of the hotel in company with the personable fur-trapper.

Whenever we caught one of these crafty customers she'd be shocked to find she'd made a mistake, "picked up the wrong coat." We seldom bothered to turn them in because they usually had money enough to hire the kind of lawyers who seemed to be able to arrange for endless postponements of the case and a house detective earns his money by being in the hotel, not in some draughty court-house corridor.

Bag-snatchers were more numerous and much harder to detect; they needed no buildup for their thievery. All they had to do was circulate around the lobby, spot a handbag that had been laid down momentarily by its owner and let human nature take its course. If the victim took her eyes off her valuables for an instant, at the Mail Desk where many women lay down their handbags while opening letters or telegrams, or at a phone booth where a person may need both hands to leaf through the pages of a phone book, the bag would do a fast disappearing act.

If, as was ordinarily the case, the bag-snatcher had come equipped with a coat to throw over the stolen bag, it was often impossible to spot the thief or recover the property. There was frequently the added difficulty that the theft had taken place where no House Officer *could* have prevented it, in the ladies' room. Some daring bag-snatchers worked the *Ladies* exclusively and in at least one case I knew of, made more money out of the lavatories than the hotel took from the coin boxes on the booth door.

Her name was Josephine; her bail bondsman, who knew her better than I did, called her "Johnny" Josephine—so I'll call her that, too. She was about twenty-two, really an elegant eyeful. Tall and slender, she looked like a Park Avenue pretty who'd "come out" after a fashionable finishing school background. As a matter of fact, she was a bright, dark-haired, dark-eyed Greek kid with no education beyond the seventh grade . . . and what she'd picked up around the *Ladies*.

From what she told me, she stuck strictly to her Johnnies, making the rounds of a dozen leading hotels every couple of weeks, never operating in one hotel more than once a fortnight.

She worked alone, was careful about picking her time. She avoided the rush hours at noon, around dinner and especially the swarming confusion of after-theater crowds.

I heard about her two or three months before she was finally nabbed. One of our washroom attendants, an elderly Irish woman, brought a complainant to my office. The complainant was a registered guest, otherwise the hotel wouldn't have had any real responsibility, though of course we'd have done what we could to recover her property.

It was about three in the afternoon. The guest, a young matron from Greenville, South Carolina, had been lunching late in the Coffee Shop, had found it necessary to visit *Ladies* on the mezzanine. The attendant hadn't been in the lavatory at the time, nor had the guest seen anyone else there. At least she hadn't seen anyone but the girl who'd stolen her handbag with some sixty dollars, driver's license, car keys, etc. in it. All she'd seen of the thief was ankles.

The guest had been in one of the stalls, having paid her admission to the coin-operated locking device. There had been some girl in the adjoining booth when the guest had gone in hers. A few minutes after the guest had entered, her unseen neighbor had opened her door, gone out to the row of washbasins and mirrors.

It was only a moment after that when the guest heard something tinkle on the tile at her feet . . . a pearl earring. At the same time the unseen girl had said: "Oh! Damn! My earring," had come close to the door of the guest's cubicle and stooped down, groping. The guest was bending over to retrieve the earring when she saw the girl's ankles and groping fingers.

"Here it is," the guest called, having recovered the bauble.

"Oh, swell!" Evidently the girl had straightened up for her hand was no longer in sight through the space below the stall door. "Just slide it out, will you . . . ? Thanks . . . terribly obliged . . . damn thing keeps coming loose all the time."

In another moment the girl was gone. It was perhaps two or three minutes before the guest realized that her handbag, too, was gone. She'd hung it by its strap handle on the hook* fixed inside the door; since there'd been no one else in the lavatory, it was clear the unseen girl had simply reached over the top of the door, taken it.

Without a description of the girl, we had nothing to go on; I had to tell our guest there was no likelihood of our recovering her property.

I was wrong; it was turned in at my office by one of the bellmen within half an hour. It had been picked up on a shelf in one of the pay phone booths at the rear of the lobby. No one remembered what the girl, who must have left it there, looked like. Everything except the money

* The activities of Johnny Josephine may have been one reason why many lavatories in public places are substituting shelves for hooks. But a tall girl with long arms can reach a shelf, too. D.C.

was intact; the guest was so glad to get back her license and car keys, she didn't press the matter of the missing money.

I notified the Hotel Association that a slick lavatory worker had made a haul, but I didn't know just how slick Johnny Josephine was until a month later when another complaint came in.

This time it wasn't a guest, but a stout, middle-aged lady who'd stopped in for a look at some embroideries on display in the lobby. She lost considerably more than sixty dollars, though she hadn't bought any embroideries.

Again, the victim had seen no one, unless a pair of shapely ankles could be called someone. The method had been about as before, but in addition to the dropped earring something new had been added, a length of twine.

The stout lady had been more alert than the South Carolina woman, had noticed the absence of her alligator bag a split second after the earring had been slid back to its owner beneath the stall door. The stout woman had yelled "Here! Stop! Thief!!" and in a matter of seconds had yanked at the knob of her door. The door had opened an inch or so, and that was all. She was penned up.

She shouted her head off. After three or four minutes, another woman, coming in, had rushed to the trapped victim's rescue by unloosening one end of a length of twine which had been looped around the handles of two adjoining stall doors. The one next the stout lady's had been locked, having been unoccupied; no amount of pushing on the door had been able to budge it.

The unfortunate lady had arrived at my office in what is often described as a "state." She was boiling mad at the indignity, demanded to know what the hotel was going to do about it.

We told her, as diplomatically as possible, there wasn't

much we *could* do about it since she couldn't describe the thief. The hotel did provide a washroom attendant during certain hours of the day. The attendant was in the lavatory from noon until 2 and from 4:30 until midnight, which was as many hours as union regulations permitted her to work.

Even the return of the alligator bag didn't mollify the stout lady, though the bag was recovered within fifteen minutes. I found it myself . . . again on the rack of a phone booth. But she didn't know how lucky she'd been to lose only her money. It might have been worse. For one of Johnny Josephine's later victims, it was.

Reports of the raids by the still undescribed thief began to multiply. They came to the Hotel Association from every good hotel in the midtown area. Only one new piece of information showed up in these later accounts; one of the victims had noticed that the thief, while standing in the stall next to the victim, had held up a small mirror in a hand stretched high over her head. Evidently this portable periscope had been used to discover whether the victim's bag had been hanging on the hook on the back of the door.

Apparently the snatcher thought she'd invented a foolproof device. At any rate, the cords which had loops tied in them in advance so it took only a second to loop one of them securely over the door handles, came into operation pretty regularly for a couple of weeks. These effectively stopped all pursuit. Eventually they stopped Johnny Josephine, too.

In one of the older terminal houses, the Johnny stalls—and hence the doors, as well—were about an inch and a half narrower than those in more modern establishments. One of these narrow Johnnies proved her downfall, because she'd failed to notice the shortened dimension and had used one of her pre-cut cords to pen a victim in her stall.

On that occasion, one end of the loosened cord whipped off the handle around which it had been looped. The victim galloped out, into the corridor, howling like a banshee. Johnny Jo began to run. A porter grabbed her.

But the snatcher had one weapon no one had suspected. Faced with her accuser, Johnny Josephine made no attempt to deny she had her victim's bag. But with downcast eyes and a shamefaced expression she murmured that she'd taken the bag because the accuser had tried to welch out on a promise to give her money . . . for sexual familiarities.

The accuser, finding herself accused of Lesbianism, was shocked speechless. Needless to say she violently denied any intimacies. But nothing would induce her to press the charge of theft. If it hadn't been for the search of Johnny Josephine's own handbag, made by the terminal hotel's Security Chief, the snatcher might have gone scot-free.

As it was, he found one of those looped lengths of twine. At least half a dozen were by that time resting in the desk drawers of other house officers all around town; it seemed likely the length in Johnny Jo's bag would prove to have been cut from the same ball of twine. So he notified the precinct and had her booked.

But there never was a conviction as far as I know. None of her victims, except the one who'd been accused of perverted familiarities, could identify Johnny Jo. If there had been others who had managed to escape from their stalls in time to grab her, it was possible they, too, had refused to make any charges for fear of being mixed up in a scandalous mess.

It's quite possible Johnny Jo's method of counter-accusation came as a result of some of her experiences in hotel lavatories, or lobbies. Because hotels, particularly the better ones, are often hangouts for Lesbians, and there's nothing much the House Officer can do to prevent it.

In hotels these off-beat she-males don't get together in groups, wearing mannish clothes, as they sometimes do in hole-in-the-wall cafés or "bohemian" eating places. But they do prowl through lobbies and lounges on the hunt for the peculiar kind of companionship they crave. Since a hotel's reputation is a delicate thing which wilts rapidly at any rumor of "queers" favoring the place, we always did what we could to discourage such goings-on.

If I noticed a woman coming to the hotel frequently, unaccompanied, seldom having appointments with men, often striking up an acquaintance with some younger girl, taking her to the cocktail lounge or dining room, a word with the headwaiter or head barman would result in the woman's getting bad service. Food would be brought to the table cold, drinks delayed and sometimes spilled. A little of that and the Lizzie, almost invariably a fastidious if not actually finicky individual, would look for other hunting gounds.

Where the aggressive Lizzie was a guest in the hotel and invited her passive partner up to her room, we would merely notify the desk, so that the next time the woman tried to register in, she would find it difficult. There were two reasons for this.

One was that jealous friends or relatives of either the Lizzie or her lady-love often caused distressing scenes in the hotel if the rendezvous was discovered. The other was that remorse, or some emotional hang-over resulting from such an affair, frequently wound up in suicide attempts, or—on at least one occasion—in attempted murder.

Many people who work in a big hotel don't work *for* it. This complicates matters for House Officers expected to keep order in parts of the house where they have little or no authority.

I've worked in hotels which leased out cigar stand, newsstand, gift shop, florists shop, travel agency, theater ticket agency, barber shop, beauty shop, laundry, dry cleaners, valet concession, public stenographer, steam baths, massage salon, drugstore, coffee shop, cafés, bars and a dozen miscellaneous stores for everything up to and including a Stock Exchange broker.

In addition, nearly every hotel (with the exception of one of the big chains) generally leases out its phone booths, the telegraph desk, also the rights to put attendants in check-rooms and washrooms. Sometimes these concessionaires are more lax about certain things than the hotel likes.

For instance, in the New York house with which I was first connected when I came to town, we began to have an unusual influx of effeminate male guests. We discovered that most of these lady-like lads were being attended in their rooms by the masseur who worked out of the hotel's famous Finnish Baths.

That sort of situation was delicate to deal with. But, rather than have the house get a reputation for being a meeting place for "queers," the management decided to ask the proprietor of the baths to fire the masseur. The operator of the baths protested. He said we had no evidence.

Faced with the possibility of court action if it tried to break the operator's lease, the Front Office put it up to me. I enlisted the services of a plain-clothes detective from the 47th Street Station, he being under some obligation to the house because of privileges extended in the dining room. He often came in for dinner with a girl friend and, as the saying went, he could have anything in the house except a check.

He was glad to oblige me by putting the arm on one of the nances who'd been calling for the masseur. All my detective friend wanted was the pansy's name. As soon as he was sure he'd been given the right name, he let the "queer" go, went upstairs to a room and phoned down to the baths.

When the masseur arrived, the detective said he'd been recommended by Blank, giving the pansy's name. Five minutes later the boss of the Finnish Baths had a phone call from that room; the masseur announced he was quitting right away; would the proprietor please check the masseur's bags and mail the check to General Delivery at the 33rd Street Post Office!

My plain-clothes pal had given him his choice of being booked as a pervert, or clearing out; he'd taken the easy way. Of course the policeman wouldn't have arrested him; that might have meant unpleasant notoriety for the hotel.

Once when the late Irvin Cobb was stopping at the house, I was having my hair trimmed in the barbershop next the one in which the Kentucky humorist was being shaved. He kept patrons and barbers alike amused with a story of World War One days.

Cobb had gone into a combination café-and-barber shop just behind the front lines in France, had been lathered and scraped by a charming young mademoiselle in a white, wrap-around apron. But when he inquired about the chances of getting a manicure, the job was tackled by a darling young chap with marcelled hair and carefully rouged cheeks!

I laughed, though possibly the story didn't strike me quite as funny as it did the others. I'd had too many difficult experiences with those girlish guys.

For the benefit of any readers who may be hep to all those statistics Dr. Kinsey collected, I might state my platform as it concerns homesexuals. I hold no prejudice against an individual who, for glandular reasons beyond his control, has impulses which aren't the same as mine. Those fellows have a tough row to hoe in life.

So none of what I have to say here refers to what I'll call the shrinking violet type of sexual unfortunate; the only trouble they've ever caused me was on a few occasions when I had to head off some loud-mouthed, hair-on-the-chest boy who'd become belligerent in the presence of an effeminate gentleman.

The ones that bothered the hotel were the aggressive pansies, the ones the staff usually referred to as "Queens." The hip-swishing, wrist-flapping type is strictly Trouble in Trousers. I've found them to be nasty-tempered and dangerously jealous.

For months I carried scars as a result of a set-to with Claudie. He and another prissy lad were in our cocktail lounge one evening, drinking, making catty and audible cracks about other patrons, and evidently on the hunt for "a friend."

First I heard of them was when Esteban strode up to me in the lobby, scowling and growling. Esteban was one of those I mentioned earlier, an employee who didn't work for the hotel. The cocktail lounge was operated by a concessionaire; Esteban had been hired by him as a strolling guitarist to sing request numbers at the tables.

He asked me to keep "those damn pansies" off his neck; they'd been making insinuating remarks every time he came near them. He'd taken all he was going to, from that pair!

I told him the head barman would tone them down— but I wasn't sure about that. That barman hated to interfere with any spenders, no matter what the provocation. So I followed Esteban back to the lounge. Right away I spotted the nances, they were dolled up like Lady Astor's horses.

Claudie, the younger of the two, flapped a hand at his waiter; when the waiter came over Claudie called out, loud enough for everyone at the surrounding banquettes to hear: "Bring us another couple of Collins . . . with Esteban on the side."

Esteban heard it. He stopped singing *Paper Moon,* stalked over with blood in his eye, snarled at Claudie: *"What'd you say?!"*

I had to step in fast. Claudie was pawing at Esteban's arm. Esteban started a punch. I barged in between them. A couple of waiters hurried over to hide the commotion from the other patrons.

While I was urging Esteban to cool off and go away, let me handle it, Claudie sprang up behind me, nearly overturning the table. I pushed him down into his seat by shoving a shoulder against him. He clawed at my face, with fingernails manicured to a fine point.

I had to grab his wrist. He bent his head, sank his teeth into the back of my hand. By the time the waiters had muscled him out to the lobby, blood was running down over my collar and onto my cuff. And Claudie was really making a scene, carrying on like some hysterical child.

For a few minutes there, I did sympathize with the he-man type who always has an inclination to sock one of the swish-sisters. But all we did was eject Claudie . . .

without giving him time to pay his check. Which made the head barman sore!

You wonder I call them Trouble in Trousers?

XIV

Sleepers and Jumpers

It would be well within the range of possibility for a baby to be born in an up-to-date, big-city hotel, and—assuming the building wasn't torn down to make way for a bigger one—grow up, get married (and maybe become a parent) without ever leaving the premises. Just about anything a person might need can be found in, or easily brought to, a metropolitan hotel. Everything, that is, except a cemetery.

I've known times when one of those would have come in handy.

Hotels are home to many lonely people; some, particularly those in the forty-to-fifty brackets, who suffer from real or imaginary illnesses, become victims of melancholia. Then the Security Office has to keep an eye on them.

What is worse, there are always a certain number of people who have decided to do away with themselves, but don't want to commit the act at home. Frequently these wind up in hotel rooms trying to decide whether to use a gun, poison, a razor blade . . . or the window. Many change their minds at the last minute. A few do get up their nerve to take the pills or the leap, but for every one who succeeds there is another who is saved, by someone on the staff, from taking his life.

Some of these would-be suicides have hysterical breakdowns after their attempts have been forestalled or blocked; then it's a matter for the house doctor or the psychiatric ward of the City Hospital. Occasionally a different type of reaction sets in, as in the case of K——, a motion-picture director.

K—— was a good-looking fellow in his middle forties, with great dark eyes brooding out through thick spectacles, and gaunt, lined cheeks. He'd come East following contract-trouble with his studio; I suppose he'd turned out a couple of flops or maybe said "No" too many times to a boss who liked to be "Yessed." Anyway he was out of a job and either broke or close to it. He was eating all his meals in his room and signing for the waiter's tips, often an indication the signer is short of cash.

He'd checked in on a Wednesday morning; I hadn't paid much attention to him beyond noticing that he seldom went out unless it was late at night . . . which might have meant merely that he didn't want to be bothered meeting people he knew.

But Sunday evening I had a call from our house doctor about him. (There are about as many suicides in hotels on Sunday as on all the other days of the week combined, whether because of the religious angle or simply that on Sunday people have more time to get moody, I don't know). When I went to the house hospital, just down the corridor from my office on the mezz, the doctor said K—— had phoned down for a bunch of sleeping pills.

"I went up to see him. I didn't like the way he looked or talked," the doctor told me. "He sounded dejected . . . said he simply had to get some sleep before he kept an important appointment in the morning. But he looked to me as if he was suffering from a severe fit of depression. I told him I'd have to make up some pills and send them up."

"Not enough to put him to sleep permanently." I didn't make it a question.

He smiled, rattling half a dozen pills in a prescription box. "If he takes all of these at once, it won't hurt him. On the other hand, if he's nervously keyed up, they might not even knock him out. In which case . . . if he has any suicidal notions . . . he might try some other method. Just thought I'd let you know."

"Has he been doing much drinking?"

"I'd say not. I think he's too down to hit the liquor."

That was about half-past eleven. An hour or so later I went up to K——'s room. The light was on, inside, but that didn't mean much one way or the other; practically all people who try overdoses of sleeping pills leave the light on. But there was quite a draft coming through the slit beneath his door; since it wasn't windy outside that probably meant he'd opened his window wide. That's something I've never known an overdoser to do.

I rapped on the door. No answer. For the space of time it took me to get out my master key and use it, I wondered if I'd delayed too long in making my checkup.

But he was there, sitting on the edge of the bed in his pajamas. He wasn't wearing his spectacles, though. People bent on suicide usually remove their glasses first.

"Beg pardon," I apologized. "Didn't realize you were still up, Mister K——. Doc told me you'd been having trouble getting to sleep. Thought I'd see if those pills had taken effect, sir."

"No," he answered gloomily, "they didn't do any good." He didn't seem pleased to see me or inclined to continue the conversation.

Still, I didn't want to walk out, leave him to whatever it was he'd been working up to. The prescription box wasn't on the bed table, by which I assumed he'd gulped all the pills, thrown the box in the wastebasket. "One of the Assistant Managers mentioned that you're in the picture business."

"I was." He gave me a short answer.

"Wonder if you could give me some advice," I went on before he could toss a "Good night" at me. "I have a daughter who's crazy to get in the movies. I keep telling her she's only one of a million youngsters who have that same goofy idea but she insists she's going to make a stab at it one of these days. What do you think of a girl's chances out there? She's all right when it comes to looks, least in *my* opinion, she has a pretty fair voice—"

"Oh, my God!" He got up, closed the window. "Why would you expect *me* to know! I've been in Hollywood nine years, and I know less about it right now, than you do!"

Well. That started him off. All I had to do was ask a simple question, he'd come back with an answer that'd take him a couple minutes to get off his chest.

To cut a two-hour conversation short, I stayed up there until he'd cussed out every nook and cranny of the picture business. I learned a lot about Mr. K—— and I wasn't kidding him a bit when I told him I thought he was a mighty interesting person.

After an hour or so, he broke out a bottle of liquor . . . and I broke the house rule about employees drinking while on duty. The scotch warmed him up a bit. He admitted he'd about come to the conclusion he was all washed up in the movies, but after thinking of all the sonzabitches out there who'd played him dirty, he'd be damned if he gave them the satisfaction of saying they knew he couldn't make the grade. He'd land another contract, show those bastards!

He was grateful enough to me for staying up there and listening to him, to promise he'd do what he could to get my daughter a screen test or at least some kind of a small part in his next picture, if she wanted to get out to the Coast. I didn't have the heart to admit my daughter was like his own celluloid creatures, strictly a thing of the imagination.

K—— was the exception, rather than the rule, however. Most of the sleeping-pill users I've had experience with were women. I've had a doorman tip me off that a certain woman waiting to be assigned a room, had given the entire contents of her purse to her taxi driver, saying, "You might as well have it as anyone else." *She* didn't get a room at our hotel, but I did get one of our Hospitality Aides to talk to the woman, who seemed erratic and possibly unbalanced.

It may seem callous to have sent such a person away, knowing she might try to "take the short cut" at some other hotel around the corner. But my first job was to protect the hotel and its guests.

The party who wants a room "high up," particularly if unaccompanied, is always subject to suspicion at the desk. If the person shows any unusual signs of nervousness or depression, the room "high up" is never available. A lack of concern about the room rate is another warning sign; the party doesn't expect to pay as she "checks out," anyhow.

Elevator men sometimes report women who have weeping spells in the cars. A woman may start down, change her mind because of others in the car who seem to be carefree and happy; she may then burst into tears and go right back up to her room. Within the next few minutes

154

a maid or perhaps the Assistant Housekeeper, will find an excuse to get in that room and size up the situation.

Phone operators catch on to some of the Sleeping Pill Beauties, hearing the caller sobbing, or overhearing some desperate farewell message. The house doctor and a nurse would be rushed to the room; a stomach pump or an emetic would undo the damage before it was too late.

Room-service waiters helped me to forestall many of the cases that never got to the Sleeping Beauty stage. A waiter would take up a tray to find the woman guest shuddering at the idea of food. (Unlike the condemned prisoner who always seems able to eat a hearty meal before walking that last mile, people with suicidal intentions shun food, though many will take a drink just before the attempt). If, in addition to refusing the ordered food, the guest seemed unusually dejected or tearful, a report would quickly find its way to the Security Office . . . and a Watch would be placed on the room.

Many times the despondent individual would try to buy sleeping pills . . . and even on occasion, poison . . . from the hotel drugstore. The bellman would be asked to make the purchase . . . and though he never did, he always made a report to my office.

Often a floormaid would sound the warning . . . as happened in the matter of the Suicide Record.

One March morning (whether it's the influence of the weather or that March 15th deadline, the third month in the year is ahead of all the others in attempts at suicide) a maid named Hazel O'Rear walked into my office holding a piece of notepaper.

"Read this, Mister Collans."

I did. It was on our own hotel stationery; it looked as if it had been scrawled by someone who'd just lost a week end or two:

155

Darling—

By the time you get this I will be where nothing
you can do will hurt me—

By the time you read this, nothing you can do will
be able to hurt

That was all the writing. "Where'd you get it, Hazel?"
"Out of the wastebasket in 1744."
"Who's the guest?"
"Girl, name of Abriski, Mister Collans. She come in
last night an' either she was a sleep-out or she didn't
do anymore'n lie down on top of the spread. She's been
drinkin' like she had to get down a gallon by Thursday.
An' she plays that crazy record over and over all the
time; she didn't even stop it while I was in the room."
"Phonograph?"
"Yes, sir. One of those portable plug-ins. I never heard
the record before, there's no words to it."
"Was she dressed when you went in the room?"
"In her slip; her dress was on a hanger." Hazel
frowned. "Maybe it's all right; maybe I should of minded
my own business, Mister Collans, but that note made me
feel creepy, I don't know . . ."
I told her she'd done exactly right. Then I got busy.
The Rack said 1744 was a Miss I. Abriski of Baltimore, Maryland. I was reasonably sure it was her right
name; nobody makes up a name like that.
The Bell Ledger said she'd checked in with only a light
overnight bag and a parcel. No record of errands to the
drugstore.
Bookkeeping had her down for a number of room-service items, sandwiches, ginger ale, cigarettes. No phone
charges.

156

I put on a pair of gray coveralls, picked up the tool box which I keep for such emergencies, went up to the Seventeenth.

The scrawl had certainly read like a couple of false tries at a suicide note, but I'd run into a few similar situations in which the writer had only been trying to frighten her boy friend or make the family feel remorseful; there'd been no attempt to carry out the threat. So I had to be careful.

I'd notified one of the Assistant Managers; he met me outside 1744. The sound of a phonograph record was faint; she evidently had the volume turned down. It wasn't any tune I recognized but Bob, the Assistant Manager, whispered:

"Hey! That's *Gloomy Sunday!*"

I remembered reading something about that; it was the Hungarian Suicide Song. A lot of people, according to the newspaper stories, had been driven to suicide just by listening to it.

Bob whispered again: "That's the one the Budapest police won't let 'em play any more. Smashed all the records they could find in the stores. *That dame must be getting set to do a high dive!*"

I motioned to him to flatten himself against the wall, out of sight when the door was open. Then I rapped and called "Electrician."

She opened the door right away. I wouldn't have described her as a beauty, but she was certainly supercharged. Her eyes were as big and black as demitasses; she walked with a kind of springy bounce; her voice was high and taut and almost hysterical. If I hadn't known about her ordering cigarettes I'd have thought she was high on reefers.

157

She'd have been about twenty-five. Her figure was better than her features and the slip she had on didn't hide much of it.

I walked right in, swinging the tool box, leaving the door wide open, but she came around behind me and closed it.

I went into my phony explanation: "There's a short along here somewhere, miss; it's overloading the whole circuit; might cause a fire. I'll have to check all the receptacles and sockets. Hope it doesn't disturb you . . ."

She said it didn't make a bit of difference to her; she hoped the music wouldn't bother *me*.

That gave me an opening. "I'll have to take that plug out to test the amps; it'll stop the machine for a while. What's that you got on there? That's quite a number."

She said something I couldn't understand; it wasn't *"Gloomy Sunday,"* though.

I went toward the writing desk, began to unscrew the bulb out of the standing lamp. I noticed she'd made a little pile of jewelry on the bureau: compact, wristwatch, earrings, a bracelet. She still wore one ring; I thought it was a small solitaire, it was on the right finger to have been an engagement ring.

Now, one of the surest indications of a genuine attempt at self-destruction by jumping is the collection of valuables intended to be left behind in the room after the leaper has gone out the window. So I was figuring on staying right there until I was sure she wasn't going to be a headline in the evening editions.

On the writing desk was a stamped and addressed envelope. The letter was for Mr. Peter Z——, on Stoll Street in Baltimore.

I set my tools on the floor as a sign I'd be right back,

said: "I'm going to have to test through from the other side" and went out to the corridor.

Bob and I went down to 1740, which was unoccupied. I wrote Peter Z——'s name and address on a card, told Bob to get our Chief Operator and give her the whole setup. My idea was, if our switchboard could get through to Mr. Z—— and let him know what was brewing, maybe he'd get on the phone and talk to the girl, talk her out of it.

When I went back to 1744 the record was still going. She was leaning on her elbows on the table with her chin in her hands, drinking in that weird music.

"Excuse me," I said, and pulled the cord on the portable. The phonograph stopped, but she began to hum right where the disc left off.

I tried to make small talk with her about the weather while I fooled around with my dummy voltmeter, but she wasn't interested. All she wanted to know was, would it be long before she could start the phonograph again.

"Hard to say. Be as quick as I can, miss." I sneaked a look at the record. The gold lettering around the hole in the middle was in Hungarian, all right: *Szomoru Vasarnap*. I couldn't see any other record around anywhere.

"That the only record you brought with you, miss?"

She said it was the only record she wanted; she was getting peevish at my clumsy poking around; maybe she suspected I wasn't an electrician. As soon as she could she started that damned record again.

I began to get the feeling it was a contest, to see which of us could outlast the other. She on edge, waiting for me to clear out; me fumbling around with bulbs and plugs and connections. If there'd been any way to test the voltage in the atmosphere of that room it might have been higher than that in the wires.

After more than half an hour I gave up on any hopes the girls on the switchboard had been able to locate Mr. Z———. I went to the phone to call the Electrical Repair Shop to get a couple of *real* workers on the job . . . and nearly dropped the phone when the bell jingled just as I touched the receiver.

A man's voice—a deep, gruff, bass voice was cooing "Ilena" in my ear!

I held out the phone. "For you, I guess."

She came over to take it, moving like someone sleep-walking.

I couldn't understand a word of what followed. The Chief Operator told me that they had both been talking in Polish. That had been the cause of the delay. Peter Z——— didn't speak English. They'd had to find one of our waiters who could speak Polish, before they'd been able to get across to Peter what they wanted him to do.

He'd come through in fine style, once he'd understood. He and Ilena had been engaged, had quarreled. She'd threatened to kill herself but he'd paid no attention. An old story, with the old satisfactory "it's all made up" ending . . . plus one new twist.

Before I left that room, she took the record off the portable, handed it to me.

"So you will not forget me," she said with tears in her eyes, "and so you will know I never forget you."

I had to dig the record out of my file a while ago, to make sure how to spell *Gloomy Sunday* in Hungarian. But I never play it.

Not that I'm superstitious. I've just had all I can take of that particular record.

XV

Screams in Suite Sixteen

SOMEWHERE in the next hotel room you occupy will probably be a neatly printed placard bearing, among other notices, one something like this:

The placing of packages on window ledges is expressly prohibited. Any violation of this rule shall operate to make the guest or tenant liable for any damages and also for all expenses incident to the defense of damage suits arising from such violation.

If you should think a warning like that too obvious to be needed, you'd be wrong. The things I've known people to leave on window ledges of hotels would make a list covering two of these pages. Shoes, particularly women's shoes just dressed with white polish, books, bottles, glasses, hats and hairbrushes are perhaps the most common articles to come plummeting down on the head of the unwary pedestrian or the top of the parked taxi.

When that happens, it may be up to the Security Staff to find out what room the missile came from. It's astonishing, when you attempt to track down a size 5A shoe which has dented a Panama hat or a Cadillac's hood, to have the owner (a) admit the footgear is hers and (b) deny that she left it anywhere near the window sill! She just can't imagine how that shoe came to fall out of the window!

Unless the falling object can be traced to a guest's

room, the hotel may be liable for damages. Consequently, maids, bellmen, room-service waiters, etc. are all instructed to remove any article from window sills. It's taken about a generation for the traveling public to learn that while it may be all right to dry out the newly washed hairbrush on the window sill at home, it doesn't workout so well where a gust of wind can whisk the brush off to a ten-story fall.

Accidents of whatever description have shown a marked decrease in hotels in recent years; it's no exaggeration to say that today the metropolitan house is actually the safest place on earth. Still, there'll always be nearsighted people who trip over rugs and exhilarated guests who'll do an involuntary cancan on marble steps. The house officer's concern with such things is to make sure the management isn't victimized by fraudulent claims.

The man who insists he slipped on some grease which the hotel should have cleaned up, may get a verdict in court unless some employee is prepared to testify honestly that only a moment after the accident, he was on the spot where the man fell . . . and that he saw no grease.

The woman who sued the Boston hotel, which employed me, might have convinced a jury that the jostling she received in one of our crowded elevators had caused her to have a miscarriage, suffer intense mental anguish and so on . . . if I hadn't checked back on her bill, found a $6.00 charge for Services of House Physician.

On the back of her card in our House Doctor's Patient File was a notation that the lady had been treated for a sprained back, etc., due to a fall sustained when getting off a Fifth Avenue bus and slipping on wet pavement!

Then there was the old lady, a rich old maid with a taste for litigation, who threatened suit for damage to her nervous system, allegedly caused by another guest's Pekinese yapping at her legs in the corridor outside her room. The hotel's attorneys took enough depositions from various members of the staff to prove that the *grand dame's* nervousness had been so bad before the incident that *nothing* could have made it worse. She checked out, but she didn't sue.

Pets were always a trial and a tribulation, though. All hotels hate pets in the rooms, but some have to put up with them. At one time, my Boston house had so many unpleasant incidents in connection with dogs that each guest bringing one into the hotel was required to sign a guarantee to repay the management in case of damage or litigation.

Dogs had to be kept leashed and, in summer, muzzled in corridors and lobbies. They weren't allowed in dining rooms, coffee shops or lounges. They had to ride in the Service Elevator when being taken for the Walk.

We had one woman who owned an Afghan, a handsome animal which had never caused any disturbance *whatever,* she claimed. But every time she'd go out, leaving the dog in the room, he'd go into a frenzy of moaning and howling.

It was no use for a bellman or a House Officer to go in and try to quiet the brute; the minute anyone came into the room, when the owner wasn't there, that Afghan would go for the intruder. After one of the maids had been bitten, the owner gave the animal away.

One couple, returning from a vacation, even brought in a baby skunk. It had, they explained, been de-skunked; there was no danger of any offensive odor. There wasn't, either, until the afternoon the critter died! Then I had to let myself in with a master key, have the carcass removed.

Use of the master key was made necessary because the

couple wanted to make sure no employee got into the room during their absence. In addition to the guest key, which unlocked only one room, there were passkeys for the maid which opened any of the fourteen rooms in the block she was supposed to "make up." Also, there was a Housekeeper's Key which would open any room on the floor; in hotels where there were Floor Clerks it was called the Floor Key. Then there were two more kinds of passkeys, a Master, which would unlock any door in the house, except those which had been locked on the inside, and a Grand Master which took care of *that* contingency.

If, after locking his door, a guest became so ill he couldn't get out of bed, I had to go up and use the Grand Master. If a guest didn't pay his bill and was considered a bad credit risk, while he was out one of the Assistant Managers would lock his room with the Grand Master; then nothing but the GM would let the guest back in to his belongings.

We had to use that emergency GM once on the room where the guest permitted a pair of Love Birds to fly around her room while she was out. A maid would open the door to take in clean linen and *whoosh*, those birds would be swooping along the corridors, flying into elevators, flapping around in the rooms of other guests.

Canaries in cages, parrots and macaws were no great problem if kept caged. But in winter, with the windows closed, any bird makes a room smell bad, and it takes a lot of airing to get the smell out of draperies, carpeting and upholstery.

The one kind of pet never tolerated in any hotel is the cat. So many people have an uncontrollable dislike for cats that a house can't afford to let them in. No cats, no kittens, however "harmless" and cute. In recent years,

164

since doctors discovered many people are allergic to feline fur, the rule has been enforced pretty strictly.

But folks who dote on cats weren't always inclined to take such restrictions seriously. So all hands had to be on the alert for smugglers who sneaked the purrers in under coats, in dress boxes, etc., etc.

Sometimes a woman would manage to hide her Angora in her room for a few days before we found out about it. There was Mrs. L——, a bright-eyed spry old girl with a mind of her own and a tongue to go with it. How long she'd had her Persian in the hotel, I never did find out.

One morning late, a floormaid reported she'd heard loud meows from one of the fourth floor rooms, either 410 or 412-14, which was Mrs. L——'s parlor-bedroom-and-bath. The maid was one of those individuals in mortal terror of all cats; she refused to go into any of those rooms.

So I went up. I couldn't hear any meowing. After knocking at the 412 door and getting no answer, I let myself in. No kitty, in bedroom, bathroom or closets.

When I went out to the elevator I heard something behind the stair door, however. It was Mrs. L——, down on the Third-floor landing, crooning "Preshy? *Preshy . . . ?* Kittykittykitty . . . C-o-ome, kitty."

I asked her if she'd lost anything. She owned up, with a touch of defiance. *Precious* must have slipped out of the closet where she always put him when she left her suite. Probably a bellboy had opened the closet to hang up a dress which had come back from the dry cleaners, had let the Persian get out without knowing the cat had been in there.

But *Preshy,* she assured me, was perfectly harmless!

I rounded up a couple of porters, had them poking into

165

every linen closet, broom closet, tub room (where mops are rinsed, etc.) and stair well. All bellmen and room-service waiters were warned to be on the lookout.

But nobody saw, or heard from, that cat.

I even set the kitchen staff to hunting through pantries, storage rooms and scrap closets, on the theory the damned animal must be starving.

Finally I asked Mrs. L—— if *Precious* was a Tom. No. *Preshy* was a lady.

I rang up the SPCA. Inside an hour a man in a post-man-gray uniform walked in carrying a pet-box with wire-mesh ends through which I could see white fur and green eyes.

It was then about three in the afternoon. I fed that stray Tom, a great big buster he was, too, with jowls like a lion cub, on filet of sole Marguery and the leavings of crab cakes Maryland. Then I let him loose on the fourth floor corridor near Mrs. L——'s suite.

He didn't seem to care much for his new surroundings, I suppose they lacked the rich smells of whatever alley he'd been "rescued" from. But he wasn't frightened. He stalked back and forth swishing his tail, muttering what sounded like uncomplimentary cat-talk. After a bit of that, he sat down and washed himself.

I began to think I wasn't so hot as a cat hunter.

But after five minutes of fur-licking, the Tom raised his head, pricked up his ears . . . and swaggered, tail up, over to the door of 416-18. He put his nose to the open-ing beneath the door . . . sniffed . . . and made that low rumbling noise tomcats make when they're interested in what's on the other side of the fence.

Room 416 was another parlor-bedroom-and-bath suite occupied by a Mr. and Mrs. Hoadley. I didn't know whether either of them were in or not.

The Tom rumbled again.

From somewhere in Suite Four-sixteen came a thin, wailing screech. The unmistakable keening of a female cat in heat. And instantly, rising high over it, the shriek of a terrified woman.

It was amplified considerably before I could get to the door, scoop up the Tom, knock and call:

"House Officer, Mrs. Hoadley."

She had that door opened fast. "There's a cat!" she gasped. "Right here in MY ROOM!" She backed away, goggling at the Tom, which was trying to get out of my arms. "Or . . . was it *that* cat?!"

I said I thought there *was* another cat in her suite; if she'd leave for a minute, I'd try and get hold of the animal. I couldn't see the Persian; the keening wasn't repeated.

When she hurried out, I phoned down to the kitchen for Mrs. L——; she'd been down there hunting for *Precious*.

The old lady hurried right up. *"Preshy, Preshy darling . . . !"*

Preshy mewed pitifully. She was under the bed but she didn't want to come out. Mrs. L—— went down on her stomach, on the carpet, reached under the bed, hauled out a bedraggled Persian.

The Tom snarled, used his claws on me. I got nicely scratched up as my reward for tracking down the female of the species.

Part of my reward, I should say. For though Mrs. L—— checked right out, since we couldn't run the risk of *Preshy's* roaming loose again, she was grateful enough to send me a present.

It was a box of fifty clear Havanas. I'd smoked the last one before those scratches had healed completely.

167

XVI

Clippers and Cheaters

ALONG ABOUT TEN every evening the head cashier of a large metropolitan hotel will stack away in the Front Office safe the day's cash receipts, anywhere from $40,000 to $75,000. For every dollar in that stack there'll be a sharpshooter dreaming up some scheme to put over a fast one on a hotel.

No Security Staff could hope to beat this army of clippers without a lot of help. Most of this comes from other employees working in what amounts to an espionage network familiar with the methods used by such gentry. But there are certain devices which assist those employees. Such as the Red Plug.

Some years ago the Right Honorable Horace Bruggley, Esq., M.P., etc., arrived in New York from London with the purpose of concluding an export arrangement with some American firms. He took a three-room suite in the hotel with which I was then employed, proceeded to do some high-level entertaining. His room-service liquor charges began to mount up, impressively.

After a week of fairly constant festivities in the M.P.'s elaborate quarters, the deals were completed satisfactorily and H. Bruggley, Esq., etc., checked out. On his bill, naturally, was quite a batch of phone charges . . . including several transatlantic tolls. But the M.P. balked at two items for New York-to-London person-to-person calls totaling $189.00. He could recall no such conversations.

When the charge slips were presented to verify the amounts, he was more mystified than ever . . . and even less willing to pay. He'd never heard of the individuals to whom the calls had been made in his name.

Indicating the dated time-stamp on the charge slip, I inquired if the Britisher had been entertaining a number of people in his suite at that particular hour.

Yes indeed, he recalled. It had been a memorable party.

I had to point out that presumably one of the exhilarated guests had slipped into one of the suite's bedrooms and put through the toll calls while their host was busy pouring Scotch and soda or gin and It out in the living room.

Reluctantly he admitted this might have happened. But, since he didn't have the remotest suspicion which of his acquaintances could have played such a scurvy trick on him, he could see no possibility of being reimbursed if he should pay the hotel. So would we be good enough to cancel the $189.00?

The management didn't want to antagonize a good patron and agreed to absorb the charge itself. This, and other similar incidents, brought about the use of the Red Plug.

The phone-drunk is a familiar problem in any hotel. A certain type of individual seems to gravitate toward the telephone as soon as he's had "one over the eight." The party with whom he longs to speak will invariably be halfway across the continent and frequently has to be roused out of sound slumber due to the difference in time, which the intoxicated character has neglected to take into account.

Almost always such a cross-country or transocean conversation is maudlin and meaningless. Occasionally one of our switchboard girls, listening to the quality of the connection would become aware of the unintelligible speech at our end of the line and would manage to break it up before the charges began to resemble the cost of a pair of ringside seats at a championship bout.

But with some 20,000 calls going through the hotel switchboard every day it would be asking too much to expect the operators to stop all calls of that nature. So the girls fix, to the plugs of phones in rooms where the liquor is known to be flowing freely, little colored tabs. These Red-marked Plugs warn operators, who may just have come on duty, not to accept long-lines toll charges without positive proof the caller is actually the registered guest.

I remember one regular patron, a wealthy lumberman from the West Coast, who asked us to put a Red Plug on his phone with a rather unusual restriction.

He'd come to New York for a couple of days of business conferences followed by a three or four-day spree. In his cups he'd call up a lot of people in Oregon and Washington. He never recalled having made any of the calls; he never protested at paying the charges. But after one such lost week end he asked us to put a Red Plug on his room for his own protection.

Seemed he was the sort of belligerent bucko who, when drunk, liked to call up people and insult them. It meant too much subsequent apologizing to square things after a spree . . . I got the idea he'd gone so far as to alienate some fairly important people out in his section of the country. Anyhow, his scheme was simple:

Once that Red Plug was on, our operators were to be "unable" to make any long-distance connections for him unless he was sober enough to remember the license number on the car his wife drove, back in Washington. He always drew a blank on that, unless he was reasonably sober!

Not even the most watchful operator can do much about fraudulent *incoming* calls. Such as the notorious case of General N——:

The General was a man of wealth and influence; chairman of the board of a nationally famous corporation. He hailed from a midwestern city we'll call Indianapolis; on his frequent visits to New York he was a privileged and popular guest at our hotel.

One morning a long-distance call came in from Indianapolis; General N—— wished to speak to the Resident Manager. The R.M. being in Bermuda for a two weeks vacation at another hotel in which he had an interest, the caller consented to talk to the Reservation Manager, Frank Heflin.

"Frank," said the voice from Indianapolis, "I'm flying to New York on Monday . . . get in around the middle of the afternoon. I want the same rooms I had last time. Can you fix me up for a week?"

Heflin was flattered at being on a first-name basis with the General; he was delighted to be able to accommodate a guest who wanted a week's reservation at $90 *per diem*. He certainly *could* fix the General up! Was there anything else he could do to accommodate the General?

"Yes, there is, Frank. My old friend, Colonel Juntizo, is flying up from Mexico City to complete some business arrangements with my corporation. If he should check in before I get there, look after him, like a good fellow."

Heflin said he certainly would.

Monday afternoon the Colonel arrived at the hotel with a raft of luggage. He was a quietly reserved gentleman of Castilian accent, formidable moustaches and the preoccupied air of the man of affairs. He seemed annoyed to find the General wasn't already in the house, the more so because he wished to cash a check on a Mexico City bank and needed the money before morning.

Heflin, anxious to please, assured him the General would probably be along in a short time; then there'd be no difficulty about funds since the General was well known to the hotel.

The General didn't arrive; instead, another long-distance call came from Indianapolis; it was taken by Heflin. An unforeseen conference had delayed the General's take-off. He'd have to put off his departure until the next afternoon. Meantime, had his friend, Colonel Juntizo, reached New York safely?

Heflin said the Colonel had arrived, but, before switching the call up to the General's suite, he mentioned the matter of the Colonel's check . . . would it be all right to cash it? From Indianapolis came amused assurance that the Colonel's check would be good up to and including six figures before the decimal; the General would guarantee it absolutely.

After the call was switched upstairs to the Colonel, Heflin reported to the Credit Manager. General N——— had said the Colonel was okay for any reasonable amount.

An hour later the hotel was poorer by $3750 and the fake Colonel was richer by that amount, less whatever split he had to make with the voice which had imitated the General's, out in Indianapolis. By the time I was notified that the check was n.g., there was no trace of the man with the moustaches.

Since then few checks have been okayed in *that* house on anyone's phoned say-so!

Much more useful than Red Plugs, when it came to clippers anxious to take the cash and let the Credit Manager worry, were the Red Cards in our Guest History files. In hotels with which I've been connected, these warning cards have many times been worth their weight in hundred dollar bills.

Every guest has a card in the History file. If you've ever stopped at a big hotel, your name will be there with the rest. Assuming you've been a reasonably good patron, your card will be White, will carry nothing more on it than the date of your previous patronage, the price of the room you had, the amount you spent and any preferences or complaints you may have expressed at the time.

Should you happen to be a VIP, or a patron of long standing . . . having stopped at the house, say forty or fifty times . . . you may be honored with a Blue card, indicative of your Blue Ribbon status. But if you ever (a) departed with any valuable hotel property in your luggage (b) skipped without paying your bill or (c) bounced a *gutta percha* check on the Cashier's wicket, you'll be marked with a Red Card.

Cross-indexed with these Red Cards are often a number of others bearing the various aliases the clipper has been known to use when defrauding other hotels. Sometimes these aliases are supplied by the Burns Detective Agency which operates under contract to the American Hotel Association and constantly circularizes names and descriptions of all known clippers and skippers.

On the Red Card, following a detailed description of the clipper's appearance, manner of dress, habits, etc., etc., will be a notation of the method the crook has employed. Here is one which was circulated for some months until I helped remove the gentleman from circulation:

T—— F——, registers single. Generally stays three or four days. Pretends to be sales rep. of firm selling retail stores. When paying bill offers check made out to him by well-known local store, usually in amount of $250 to $300. Mentions names of company executive. Check is on good imitation of tinted bank stock, printed with name of store, perforated with check-protecting device, signed and countersigned, with rubber-stamped endorsement clause on reverse. F—— also presents letter on facsimile store letterhead, apparently forwarded to him by mail at the hotel, referring to check transmitted "herewith." Never shows envelope, not liable for mail fraud. If apprehended, hold and notify . . . . etc., etc.

This gentleman took his pitcher to the well once too often, while I happened to be within hearing. He was trying to pay his bill, amounting to $46 or so, at the busiest time of day, quarter to six in the evening.

He had the letter from one of the biggest Fourteenth Street stores, and the check which was mentioned in the letter. The name on check and letter wasn't the one on his Red Card, or on any of the cross-reference cards. It was a brand-new one, coined especially for us.

He *looked* all right. He *sounded* all right. His credentials were perfect. If it hadn't happened that I'd been going over the Association flyers the evening before, I'd never have suspected him, myself. As it was, I played it cagey by being apologetic when I asked him to step up to my office.

He made a mistake then by trying to make a run for it. I didn't have to be apologetic then, and wasn't.

You might remember that character, next time you're inclined to resent what you think is a haughty stare from the desk clerk who seems to be trying to decide whether you're worthy of the double with twin beds which you've requested. In all likelihood, the clerk is simply trying to remember whether you bear any resemblance to the characters described on those Red Cards in the Guest History Files.

While I'm on that topic, there's another habit of hotel personnel which may have annoyed you if you've ever tried to cash a check without having a hotel Credit Card. You may remember that, if you did succeed in getting the Credit Manager's okay, it took you quite a while to convince him no matter how much identification you may have had with you in the shape of car license, lodge memberships, Social Security or Honorable Discharge from the Armed Forces.

The reason for that would have been that any crook is bothered by delay in putting over a fast one. The longer it takes, the more chance there is that someone will recognize him or get wise to him. Hence the Stall.

The clipper trying to cash a piece of worthless paper often gets nervous at being made to wait. Sometimes he starts to sweat, his palms, particularly. The Credit Manager will be watching closely for any such signs of apprehension.

If he did okay your check, probably he walked part way to the Cashier's window with you, possibly he took the check to the Cashier himself to be translated into folding money. You may have supposed this was an act of courtesy, amends for having made you wait. It was simply a precaution to see that you didn't pause somewhere to copy his scrawled signature or initials. One of the favorite tricks of clippers is to get a *good* check okayed in order to duplicate that okay which may then be forged on a later and worthless piece of paper.

When you stop to think that one hotel chain alone cashes about a million dollars worth of checks a week (almost all on the strength of its own credit cards), it's easy to understand why there are always a lot of clippers trying to slice off a small piece of that total by unlawful means. It's old stuff to say that the ingenuity some of them spend on cheating hotels would not only earn them a good living if it were applied legitimately, it's also an understatement. It would make them rich.

Take Harald Myrtenson as a prime example.

My acquaintance with this curious clipper began when I had a call from our housekeeper; she had something she wanted to show me. A pillow slip stained with green ink, bright blue-green.

"When I asked the maid about this," the Houskeeeper said, "she told me the gentleman in 809 must have been cleaning his fountain pens on it."

"Pens, plural?"

"That's what made me wonder," the Housekeeper answered, "so I asked her again. According to her, the gentleman spends most of his time in his room writing, with a dozen pens."

"Maybe the guy's a fountain pen salesman. Or an inventor trying out a new kind of ball point." But I began to check around on the guest in 809.

The card in the Rack said he was Harris Morse of Binghamton, New York, single, $6.50 rate. In the house five days.

Bookkeeping said he'd had a number of local phone calls, a quantity of laundry charges, a normal amount of room-service, mostly breakfasts, very little liquor.

Credit had nothing on him; H. Morse was not on our Credit Approved list nor had he asked to have any checks cashed.

The room-service waiter who generally took up the breakfast tray to 809 was Heinrich, a fat, stolid German.

He could tell me nothing about Morse except that the man tipped in cash, not liberally but all right.

It was then eleven-thirty in the morning. Heinrich had taken the room-service table and dirty dishes down from 809 long before, but I sent him back upstairs anyhow with orders to say a sugar bowl had been missing; maybe Mr. Morse had forgotten to put it back on the table . . . ?

When Heinrich reported back to me he had some odd information. "Six, seven bottles of ink he's got on the desk, Mister Collans. Green ink, blue, black, red, couple different kinds of red. And a bunch of pens."

I asked what Morse had been using all the writing materials for . . . ?

"Search me, Mister Collans. They wasn't no notepaper on the desk blotter nor nothing else, as I could see."

"No checks?"

"No sir. Not a thing."

Now there's no law against a guest's playing with pens and ink, still . . .

I thought about it awhile. After lunch, I sent the floor-maid around with instructions to use her passkey, bust right in as if she thought the guest was out of his room, then apologize and use her eyes.

She came down to my office in ten minutes to say she'd done what I'd told her to and it had made the guest good and sore. He'd been working at the desk with some kind of machine; he'd jumped up the instant she'd opened the door, bawled her out, waved his arms excitedly, shoved her back into the corridor.

I asked what the machine had looked like.

She hadn't had a very good look at it, couldn't say.

Might it, I suggested, have been a printing press?

She'd never seen a printing press that small; it might have been one, though.

177

My probing attempts must have alarmed Morse because he went into action fast. About quarter past two I had a cryptic call from the Credit Manager; would I drop right down?

I did, to find Mister H. Morse sitting there calmly in the chair beside the C.M.'s desk. The latter was on the phone to a bank in Albany, New York.

"I have a Mister Harris Morse in my office," our credit man was saying, "he wants us to cash a certified check issued by your bank . . . three hundred and fifty . . . that's right . . . dated last Friday . . . oh, I see . . . yes . . . well, thank you very much indeed, sir . . . No, no . . . no difficulty . . . merely checking, we're not acquainted with Mister Morse . . . that's all . . . much obliged." He hung up

Morse eyed me coolly. I looked inquiringly at the Credit Manager, who touched a check on the desk before him.

"Bank says it's okay; they issued this cashier's check to Mr. Morse last Friday." He turned the check over, scribbled his initials on it. "You understand we have to be careful on matters like this, Mister Morse."

Morse said he appreciated that; it was quite all right.

"Mister Collans will take you to our cashier." Our C.M. held out his hand. "Hope you'll stop here again, next time you're in town, sir."

"Thanks, I will." Morse shook his hand.

Everything seemed according to Hoyle. But this sudden maneuver to get hold of cash, coming so soon after what might have been clumsy attempts to find out what Morse had been doing, made me wonder. I couldn't get over the feeling something was wrong.

He must have felt I was suspicious because when he

came down with his luggage, a suitcase one of the bell-men was carrying and an old tan Gladstone he hung onto himself, he scarcely gave me a glance.

He climbed into a cab, told the driver to take him to Penn Station.

I was still absent-mindedly staring out at the street ten minutes later when that same driver slid his taxi into our cab rank. *It took a good twenty minutes for a hacker to get from our hotel down to the Pennsylvania Terminal and back!* Morse must have changed his mind suddenly.

I went out. Sure, the driver said, he hadn't gone more'n a couple of blocks when his fare had decided to stop at a bank on Madison Avenue before going to his train. The driver had collected a good fat tip for setting the gentle-man on the sidewalk only three blocks from the hotel.

I made it over to the bank fast. Morse was sitting next the desk of one of the Vice Presidents, behind the marble railing. He saw me come in; I thought he looked panicky.

I told the gray-uniformed bank guard who I was and what I wanted He took me in through the gate in the railing, over to the V-P's desk.

The V-P was on the phone:

". . . I understand . . . the gentleman says his hotel wasn't able to take care of it so he—"

Morse slid out of his chair sideways. The guard grabbed him.

The V-P said to the phone . . . "If you'll hold the phone a moment, please . . ." and to the guard: "What's the trouble?"

I said: "The trouble is, the gentleman *did* cash his cer-tified check at my hotel about twenty minutes ago; I'd like to know how he's doing it a second time."

The V-P examined the Cashier's check on his blotter;

I could see he was sure it was genuine. But he did ask the man at the bank in Albany if he'd issued *two* certified checks. The answer was no.

The rest of the answer we found in "Morse's" Gladstone. A small printing press with packets of tinted and silk-threaded bank-paper blanks, tubes of ink, a check-perforating device, so on. He'd paid three hundred and fifty to the bank in Albany for a good certified check; carefully duplicated it down to the colored-ink perforations, signatures, etc., and proceeded to try and cash both the original and the duplicate.

It was the duplicate he'd worked off on our Credit Manager (no discredit to him, either, for it was a beautiful job of forgery). Knowing the hotel would check with Albany . . . and that the bank there would honestly report that such a certified check had been issued, "Morse" felt sure the duplicate would be accepted. He'd saved the genuine check for the bank, on the supposition a banker might be more likely to detect any minor flaws in paper, ink or printing.

"Harris Morse" turned out to be Harald Myrtenson, who had turned out four sets of those beautifully duplicated counterfeit certifications before our Housekeeper noticed that a pillow slip had carelessly been used as a pen wiper.

I mentioned before that if a fellow as clever as that had used his wits toward legitimate ends, he'd really have gone far. He did anyhow: after being sentenced to an upstate penitentiary he forged his own parole papers and, the last I heard, was still at liberty.

But he won't be trying to clip hotels. His name and his *modus operandi* are on too many Red Cards.

XVII

Danger—Women Working

You're not obliged to pay attention to those placards tucked beneath the glass bureau top in your hotel room, advertising sensational values at the Savile Men's Shop or the marvelous permanents obtainable at the Salon de Beauté. It may cost you some money, if you fall for them. But if you disregard those other little warnings neatly arranged between the Club Breakfast menu and Rates for Rental Limousines, it may be even more expensive.

The first of these warnings will generally be a request to *Please Keep Your Door Locked,* coupled with the information that *The Key Must Be Turned In The Lock.*

The second will notify you the management will accept no responsibility for the loss of valuables, since safe deposit boxes are available without charge at the Cashier's Office.

The third will frequently put you on your guard against phony photographers preying on out-of-town visitors.

All simple and sensible. Yet four out of five guests ignore one or more of these warnings every time they stop at a hotel. That they don't, more often, pay dearly for disregarding these suggested precautions is due to the watchfulness of Security staffs. The case of Aggie Houlan will show what I mean.

Aggie was a floormaid at the New York hotel where I was first Assistant Security Chief and later Chief. She was an Irish woman of thirty-five or so, small, quick of movement and quick of wit. An impudent snub nose, a sharp pair of black eyes, and—on occasion—an impudent tongue. It wasn't the tongue that got her into trouble, though for a while I thought it was.

She'd been working in the hotel about a month before I had any special reason to notice her. All floormaids were assigned to "sections" of fifteen bedrooms; hers was on the sixth floor. When a report came up from the desk that a guest in one of her rooms complained that an emerald bar-pin had been stolen, I dug out Aggie's Record of Employment card and phoned the Housekeeper's Office to have her come in and see me.

It was routine; I didn't really suppose she was a thief. A big proportion of "stolen" articles turn out to have been merely misplaced. Sometimes the guest will eventually remember where she put the wristwatch, or whatever, for safekeeping; occasionally she's too shamefaced to admit it, but then she stops squawking about it and we know the lost has been found. None of these things happened in connection with the bar pin.

Aggie's card said she lived on Soundview Avenue in the Bronx, had been married but was separated and was rooming with a married sister. She'd worked for the *Montclair,* before taking her job with us; they gave her a good reference. The only notation on our employee record was the Assistant Housekeeper's comment: *Gossips with guests; resents criticism.*

When she came into the office, I could understand the comments. She flattened my ears; she was burned up at the very idea of being suspected. Hadn't she always been an honest, hard-working woman! Would she be slaving over dirty bedlinen and scrubbing toilets, if she was stealing jewelry from folks too damn careless to know what they'd brought to the hotel and what they'd left at home!

She'd be thankful if I'd have her searched straightaway, if I'd have her locker searched. Sure, I could go up to the Bronx and go through every stitch and stick she owned, Lord knew it was little enough I'd have to look through. And so on. To me, she sounded as angry as an innocent person should have; I said so in my report to the Front Office.

The guest didn't find the pin. It hadn't been insured. The management reminded her tactfully of that printed warning about depositing valuables with the cashier. I didn't hear anything more about it, but of course I made my own notation on Aggie's card. It simply read *Bar Pin* and the date.

I didn't pay much attention to her for a couple of weeks. Several other "thefts" had been reported from other floors and because some of the stuff didn't turn up, either in the L & F or in the guest's recollection, we began to think there were some Walk-Ins at work.

A Walk-In is a room-rifler who finds a guest's door unlocked and just walks in, helps himself and beats it. Of course he wouldn't be able to get away with it if guests heeded that warning about keeping their doors locked. But there are certain times when even the most careful guest is likely to neglect that advice.

One of those times is right after waking up. Many hotels make a practice of shoving a morning paper partway under the door, compliments of the house. Sometimes it's the guest's home town paper. Sometimes, if the paper is a fat issue, it gets stuck under the door. About half the time, a guest, on getting up, will open the door to pick up the paper, and won't bother to lock the door when he shuts it again.

So the Walk-In strolls along a corridor, watching for

doors where there is no paper. He listens at the door; if he hears a shower running, he tries the door. When, as often happens, he finds it unlocked, he'll step in, grab whatever he sees handy, preferably a wallet or a purse off the bureau, and quietly depart while the sound of the shower covers his exit.

Sometimes the Walk-In makes his (or her) own breaks. Most room-calls, about 90 per cent of them, are for the period from 7:15 to 8:15. During this waking-hour, the Walk-In thief will prowl a corridor listening for the ring of the phone and the drowsy: "Hello" which indicates the guest is just about to get up.

A minute or so afterward, the Walk-In will rap on the door. When the guest opens it, the prowler will apologize profusely; he was looking for Eddie, terribly sorry, must have made a mistake, thought this was Eddie's room. The sleepy guest generally forgets to lock the door. He isn't used to relocking his own door at home; it doesn't occur to him to do it in a hotel.

One notorious Walk-In refused to waste his time waiting for the guest to step into the shower. This character, on making sure that a door was unlocked and the guest still in the room, would go down to the lobby, ring up the room on the house phone.

"Sorry to bother you," he'd growl, "but this is the Engineering Department. We have to cut the water off from your bathroom in fifteen minutes for emergency plumbing repairs."

Then he'd streak back upstairs, arriving at the unlocked door just in time to hear the rush of water in the shower. The rest would be like taking candy from a tongue-tied tot.

The Walk-Ins who make the biggest cleanups are generally women. They hit a corridor where the linen carts show the maids are working; usually they'll carry a package, nicely wrapped, maybe an empty hatbox.

When the Walk-In passes a room with the door open and no sign of the guest around, she'll look for some feminine articles on the bureau or in one of the chairs. Soon as she is fairly sure it's a woman's room, or a couple's, she marches right in. Often she'll be jingling a room key as if she'd had it out, ready to use, though she's careful not to put it on the bureau top where the maid might notice it's not the one for the room at all.

The Walk-In will apologize prettily to the maid for interfering with her duties. If the maid seems to be nearly finished, the Walk-In may simply put her package on the bureau and wait. Usually she asks if the maid will mind if she has the room to herself for a few minutes, to change her clothes. There's no reason for the maid to question her as the rightful occupant, so she steps out. The Walk-In carries her loot away in the hatbox.

From the nature of the stuff that was being reported "stolen" through the hotel, I was pretty sure we had a female rifler to deal with. All the missing items had been taken from the rooms of couples or of a woman guest. Not all the things that had been taken were women's things. A married man had lost a bunch of neckties (the sort of thing many female thieves latch onto and give to their boy friends), a set of onyx dress studs, a cigarette case. But all the items reported to us as stolen were small enough and light enough to go in a hatbox or a dressbox, which Walk-In women also use, on occasion.

We had all the floormaids alerted to ring the Security Office soon as any supposed guest walked in a room without actually using her key. The elevator boys were told to watch out for women going upstairs in the morning with bags or boxes or bundles and let us know right away. No results. And every few days there'd be another squawk from the Front Office about room riflers. Everybody was kind of scratchy-tempered about it.

I hadn't been paying much attention to Aggie Houlan; no more complaints had come in from her section of rooms. Then one evening a guest on the sixth let out a bellow which could have been heard all the way to the sub-basement; her leather jewel box had been forced, two diamond dinner rings stolen.

The rings were valuable, had been insured for $8,000. The guest was a Mrs. Y——, who was more or less a guest of the management. She ran a travel bureau in St. Louis, routed many of her continent-bound round-trippers into the hotel.

Mrs. Y—— had, in the past, done the hotel a great deal of good. Judging by the storm she was setting up, it was clear that in future she'd do us a good deal of harm, if her property wasn't recovered. The rings, it seemed, had a sentimental value far beyond the coverage allowed by the insurance people.

Aggie, of course, came under suspicion immediately. The maid had been in the room only a morning or so before Mrs. Y—— had opened the leather case to get a brooch, at the time had seemed curious as to the contents of the case.

One of the difficulties in a case of theft is striking the right balance between zeal to recover stolen property and loyalty to the staff. Over the years it's been my experience that nine out of ten hotel employees are, at least, as honest as bank cashiers. But right then it was a little harder than usual for me to defend Aggie's integrity as a trusted employee.

For one thing, jewels weren't the sort of loot a Walk-In woman would be able to get her hands on; she'd

186

have to take time to open the jewel case; whereas she'd have been much more likely to take the case itself. But jewels would be just the thing a dishonest maid might take. Easy to conceal on her person; easy to hold until it was safe to sell or pawn them.

When I talked to Aggie, the morning after the theft was reported, she maintained the pose of indignant innocence. It even seemed possible she was overdoing it!

"An' why should I be puttin' up with all this, for a lousy twenty-five bucks a week!" she cried, nearly as I can recall. "Bein' called a thief to my face, me that's never taken so much as a penny, wasn't mine! Treated like a common criminal, when all I've done's to get down on my knees an' scrub my soul out. Th' hell with her; she prob'ly's got them rings hidden somewheres so she can collect the damn insurance. Hell with you, too! I don't have to work for people who cover up their own short-comin's by blackeyein' an innocent woman's repettation." Aggie really poured it on.

And she quit. Turned in her uniform, called for the part-week pay due her, and went home. I thought the matter was out of my hands then, since we'd had to report the missing jewels to the precinct. We didn't have a thing on Aggie. The police couldn't hold her, either. But I knew they'd check on her, as well as keep a lookout for the rings or the unset stones, in the hock shops.

The lady-manager of the Tourist Bureau stayed on, and made life miserable for our resident manager and his executive manager, my boss. The insurance company wasn't making things any easier, since they'd stalled on paying off to Mrs. Y——. They based this, in part, on her negligence in not taking her valuables down to the safe deposit boxes at the Cashier's office. A very uncomfortable *impasse*.

187

Meanwhile, reports of room rifling continued to come in. It seemed pretty evident that, whatever else Aggie might have done, she hadn't been responsible for thefts on the other floors. That's what I thought until one of our elevator operators made a dumb, and fortunate, mistake.

He was a new boy, a West Virginian, named Levin, very eager to Make Good. Whenever I asked him if he'd seen a certain party, he'd listen carefully to my description and then exclaim that he wasn't absolutely sure but he *thought* he *had* seen that very same person, only a few minutes before. He was almost always wrong.

None of the Security staff took Levin seriously. So one morning when he reported that a young woman with a package had asked to be let off at the seventh floor —he'd seen her before but hadn't recognized her as a guest—I sent one of my assistants up to check, without any expectation of making a collar.

In a few minutes, however, my assistant showed up at the office with a good-looking young lady of twenty-eight or thirty. She had a big manila envelope under her arm. No package. Apparently Levin had figured that anything larger than a guest-size cake of soap was to be considered a suspicious bundle!

My assistant told me, *sotto voce,* that he'd asked her to come along with him, not because he thought she was a Walk-In but because she was working with one of those phony photo outfits. We'd been doing all we could, legally, to keep them out of the hotel.

These gyps (and there are plenty of them still operating) prey on the vanity of out-of-town visitors by phoning to their hotel rooms, suggesting their home town papers would be interested in having their pictures on the Society pages. Some of them go so far as to state they represent the Associated Press Photographers or the United Press Photographers, giving the impression they're connected with the big wire services. All they're connected with is rented desk space in somebody's office.

If the flattered guest consents to have his picture taken, the "press photographer" comes around, sets up his camera, uses three or four flash bulbs and asks the guest to sign a "release" . . . permitting the picture's use in the papers. An hour or so later a man will show up with a dozen crude black-and-white prints for which the guest is asked to pony up an exorbitant price.

When he puts up a protest, the photographer (a) reveals that the "release" was actually a contract to purchase the dozen prints and (b) threatens a mild form of blackmail if the guest fails to come through. This takes the shape of insinuating the photographer will file suit for the amount due and then wire the story of the suit to the guest's home town paper.

Some of these racketeers add a sex angle to the routine by sending an attractive girl around to collect. Many men will pay up to avoid being thought a cheap skate by a woman. In other cases, a more intimate form of persuasion may be used to close the deal and collect the cash.

The girl Levin had spotted looked the part. Smartly dressed. A pert face with dark eyes and a short, impudent pug nose. It reminded me so much of Aggie Houlan's nose that when I asked her name I half expected to hear her say Houlan. She said it was Martha Rohd. Then I remembered Aggie's name was her married name. I wondered if it had been Rohd before it had been Houlan.

Martha didn't seem a bit flustered. Asked who she'd been looking for she answered coolly: "Mister J. M. Harriman, Room 760." A call to the desk showed no J. M. Harriman in 760 or anywhere else in the hotel.

I asked to see the prints. She gave me the big manila

envelope. In the upper left-hand corner was printed: *Celebrigraphs, for:* and then written beneath it, *J. M. Harriman, Room 760.* The photographs inside were of a little, dried-up winter apple of a man in his sixties; I'd never seen him.

"Maybe you're barking up the wrong tree," I told her. "Why don't you let me call your office, find out if you're hunting for your client in the wrong hotel?"

She seemed flabbergasted but she gave me a number. I rang it. A man answered. I asked if he represented *Celebrigraphs.* He went away. Presently another voice came on. After a couple of questions he said J. M. Harriman was in Room 760 of the Hotel Clinton . . . which was a couple of miles away. I thanked him and told the girl.

She appeared to be disgusted with her stupidity; took the photographs and went away.

I got busy on the phone to the detective Lieutenant who'd been handling the dinner-ring case over at the precinct station. I explained that it was strictly a stab in the dark, but that a girl like the one who'd just left my office would have made a perfect Walk-In operator.

Working for an outfit which was plainly a racket and carrying that envelope to stall off any challenges as to what she might be doing in a hotel, even the wrong one, she'd have a pretty good excuse if she happened to be caught in someone's else room. She'd be waiting for the customer to show up; she'd be sure he'd have wanted her to wait until he came back, etc.

If, in addition to that card of admission, she'd been put wise, possibly by a sister, to the ropes and so would know just how the floormaids operated . . . and what to do if any of them should get suspicious, the young woman would be pretty well equipped to Walk In and help herself.

You can find the rest of it in the records of the trial at General Sessions. The Lieutenant and I went up to the Bronx, with a search warrant. (The Soundview Avenue address was the only thing Aggie hadn't lied about.) Aggie's husband was there; he was a baker who went to work at midnight. He was more astonished than we were when we found the *cache* in the nylon nailed to the back of the dresser.

Rings, cigarette cases, lighters, pins, studs, cuff links, wristwatches; it looked like the contents of a pawn-broker's window when we spilled it out on the spread of Aggie's bed.

The dinner rings were there . . . Aggie'd taken them, as well as the bar pin. Sort of a sideline while she was tutoring Sister Martha to be a Walk-In Woman. Also there were a lot of items that hadn't been taken from the guests at my hotel. Martha'd gained enough experience so she'd felt safe in trying out her wings where her older sister wouldn't be around to protect her in case she flopped. It took six months before all the owners were located.

The girls had tried to pawn a few of the items but they'd been offered so little, probably because the broker had sensed the stuff had been stolen, that they'd refused the paltry offers. Aggie admitted they'd been looking around for a "nice, trustworthy man who'd give them a fair price for the whole lot!" Well . . . I *said* she was impudent.

Anyhow, Levin's blunder and my lucky recognition of a pug-nosed facial characteristic took Mrs. Y—— off the executive manager's neck. And took him off mine.

So I felt it was no more than right to send Aggie and Martha the cartons of cigarettes every Christmas while they were out on the Island. I even put in a good word for them with the Parole Board when they wanted to be Walk-Out women.

I get a card from Aggie once in a while, even now. She's running a motel in New Mexico. Making her own beds, too.

XVIII

The Boy Hotels Hate Most

THE ONE ABOUT the hotel guest who only left his room because he couldn't get it in his suitcase is no joke to House Officers. Like most Security men, I've had to deal with so much larceny and downright destructiveness that I'm considerably soured on the honesty of the traveling public.

Under the glass top of my desk I used to keep a clipping from some newspaper column, a jingle that went:

> *Show me the guest*
> *(It won't be You!)*
> *Who never has snitched*
> *A towel or two*

Stolen towels run into big money; they vanish by the hundreds of thousands, every year . . . from any hotel in the 1000-room class.

Women take them as souvenirs. Men wrap soiled shirts or dirty shoes in them. "They make such good stuffing to pack around little things in a suitcase," one nice old lady confided to me without any embarrassment. "I don't use them at home; I have my own colored ones, which go with my bathroom. Still, I just can't resist taking hotel towels. But I must say I don't think you have as good ones as you used to when I first began to collect them, when I was a young girl."

It seems to be accepted that swiping hotel towels isn't theft at all, it's considered a mark of distinction to be able to drape over the towel rod in the summer cottage a choice collection of *Hiltons, Statlers* and *Sheratons.* Shows you've been around!

Only catch is, you may not have been around as much as the next fellow, in which case you're probably paying for some of the stuff *he's* pinched on *his* travels. No hotel can absorb the cost of 35,000 or 40,000 top quality bath towels annually. It has to be passed on to guests.

But even the most long-suffering Front Office has to draw the line at people who think it's just good clean fun to steal the blankets off the bed, the pictures off the wall and the seat and lid from the johnny. When things get to that stage, the Security Office gets a hurry call.

There was, for instance, the scion of a well-to-do Texas oil man who had the idea it was all right to get away with anything which wasn't too big to get out of his room. A good-looking, well-set-up, free-spending son of a buck, the sort of youngster people sometimes refer to as having been born with a silver spoon in his mouth. In his case it would probably have had *Biltmore* stamped on the handle.

After three days and nights of painting the town a nice lobster red, he checked out of our hotel around eight-thirty one December morning. Before he'd gotten down to the lobby I'd been notified that an ash tray stand, one of those gadgets which drop ashes down into a heavy hollow base, was missing from his room.

The moment he'd called to ask for a boy to come get

his luggage, the bell captain had notified the Rack clerk who immediately sent out, over our telautograph system multiple notifications of the room number. When the Housekeeper saw the room number, she sent a floormaid directly to the room. The first job every maid has, in a newly vacated room, is to note the condition of the hotel's property. She'd telephoned the Housekeeper the ash receiver was missing.

At first the Housekeeper thought that ash stand must have been taken out of the room for repairs; it was too big to go into anyone's hand luggage. Then she realized it was dismountable, could have been taken apart into pieces which might have been fitted into a suitcase. So she called me.

We had to go easy on people suspected of swiping stuff more valuable than a coffee spoon or a cocktail napkin. So I merely "gave the thumb" to the bellman who had the Texan's bag. When the guest had paid his bill and was looking for his luggage, I told him there seemed to have been a little mistake and that his suitcase had been taken to my office on the mezzanine. If he'd care to come with me . . . ?

He kept a tight grin on his face all the way up the stairs while I was explaining that a prank was a prank but certainly he couldn't want the $8.50, which the ash stand had cost, tacked onto his bill. He didn't deny having taken the thing; he just let me do all the talking. When I got to my office I understood why.

His suitcase was on the floor beside my desk. I hefted it; it was plenty heavy enough to have contained the ash stand's extra weight. But the suitcase was locked.

Now, not one out of a hundred guests ever locks his luggage at any time in a hotel. The assumption that he'd locked it because there was hotel property in it, was automatic. But though I pointed this out to him, he still refused to open it.

He had, he announced blandly, paid his bill. He was no longer a guest; I had no right to detain him or his luggage. If I made him miss an important appointment, he'd bring suit against the hotel.

I picked up the phone, asked to be connected with the precinct police station. He grabbed for the suitcase. I held onto it; he took a healthy swing at me.

It's a rock-bound rule that no house detective shall lay hands on a guest. But there's nothing in the book about banging him into the corner of a steel file. Somehow the back of his head bumped the jamb of the door.

In the roughhouse, his tan topcoat came open. As he sat there on the floor, he seemed to be wearing—under his tweed suit coat—a lime-green cummerbund. It was one of our new shower curtains. The maid had been so anxious to report the missing ash stand she hadn't bothered to check the bathroom.

He gave me the little key to open the suitcase, then. But the grin was off his face, and the pain from the lump on his head was bringing tears which, of course, made him madder than ever. I think he'd have liked nothing better than to mix it up some more, but by that time one of my floor patrols was in the office. Two-to-one odds toned the Westerner down.

It was just as well. Because, when I got the suitcase open and hauled the sections of the ash stand out from beneath a dinner jacket and a stack of shirts, I found something else. The glass top of one of our bed tables!

My patrolman asked the Texan why he hadn't taken the mirror out of the bureau, too, while he was at it. The youngster snapped the catches on his suitcase angrily, snuffled back his tears. With his face puckered up with rage he bawled: "Think I couldn't've paid for that stuff, don't you! I could've paid for it, all right! I could *buy* your whole goddam hotel!" He wiped his nose with one finger. "Maybe I *will*, too! An' the first thing I'll do'll be to fire you two sonzabitches!!"

To the best of my recollection no one has ever gotten away with a bureau mirror, but at one time or another I've blocked attempts to take out of a room pretty nearly everything else that's transportable. Bath mats, light bulbs, bedspreads, liquor glasses, window drapes, the silver warming domes used to keep breakfast platters warm, mattress protectors, vacuum coffeepots, faucet handles, sheets, everything from steak knives to Gideon Bibles.

Your "double with shower" in a good hotel represents an investment just about equal to the entire cost of an average eight-room house in an upper middle-class suburb. If you own such a house, or hope to, you can understand why hotels are beginning to bear down on the guest who feels that payment for a night's lodging entitles him to grab off everything he can find room for in his luggage.

The Decorating Department does what it can to prevent pilfering. It buys lamp bases too big to carry away, pictures framed so as not to fit into suitcases (the ordinary 20x30 size isn't convenient for packing purposes), bathroom fixtures which defy removal except with the aid of special tools. Towels and bath mats have the hotel's name woven-in; silverware has it stamped into every piece. But there will still be those who think it's "just a gag" to slip a pair of salt and pepper shakers into their handbag at dinner, or a pillow slip into the suitcase at the last moment before checking out.

Of course you're not that type; but if you know anyone

who is, you can tell him (or her) he isn't getting away with a thing. If he takes a bath mat, the maid's checkup will show it before he checks out. Probably the house officer won't ask him to unpack his bag and disgorge, but sometimes the value of the article will appear on the guest's bill . . . to his embarrassment. When it doesn't show up there, it'll be on his Guest History card in the files; next time he checks in . . . or wants to . . . he may have difficulty getting a room.

There are a lot of things I don't know about petty larceny of this sort. Why there's so much more in fall and winter than in spring or summer. Why women steal so much more than men, and seem so unembarrassed when called on it, and so on. But of one thing I am sure, those who swipe property aren't as much nuisance as those who damage it.

I've run into as many different kinds of destructive guests—both careless and malicious—as there are days in the year. Sometimes, during a convention, I've had to deal with fifty-seven different varieties simultaneously.

There are the Grown-Up Juveniles who squirt water pistols in the elevators, bring red flares into the lobby. The Great Big Kids who drop fireworks down over the mezzanine railing. The Convivial Boys, who've spent a little too long coming through the rye and lean too heavily on cigar counters or against lobby vitrines, those little glass showcases displaying neckties or jewelry or corsages. The Hail Fellows who tear up strip carpets, carefully laid to prevent wear in front of elevators, etc., and drape them across the sidewalk in front of the hotel to honor some newly elected Commander or Grand Panjandrum or whatever.

Up in the rooms they smash bottles, tramp gum into the carpets, get into brawls, bust up the furniture. What they do sometimes to wallpaper, floor coverings and porcelain wear is enough to keep a crew of wall washers. carpet cleaners and plumbers busy for a month after one of these riotous get-togethers.

The greatest single instrument of damage is the cigarette. In one suite, in a Boston hotel where I worked, the upholstery repair crew reported thirty-four holes in mohair and tapestry chairs and sofas after a four-day convention of a national organization well-known for its reunion *whoop-de-doo*.

It's possible to get bloodstains off a jumbo wing chair by using a paste of cornstarch, cold water and patience. Gum can be extracted from a Wilton by using plenty of ice, carbon tetrachloride and elbow grease. But all you can do with a hole burnt by a cigarette is to take the upholstery off and reweave it or replace it.

Late one winter night, smelling smoke from a corner suite occupied by four highly placed officials of a national group celebrating its umpteenth anniversary, I let myself in with my master key after getting no response to my knock.

In one of the living room chairs a gaudily uniformed guest was sprawled out with his bald head hanging over the arm of the chair. On the big Lawson sofa a younger but white-haired man in trousers and undershirt was stretched out dead to the world while the sofa cushions beneath him fumed like a town dump. A glowing circle of smouldering fabric was only a couple of inches from his trouser cuffs. The room was thick with a choking smoke.

On the center table was a litter of rum bottles, beer bottles, soda bottles, glasses and a couple of plastic tubs which had held ice. I made a dive for one of the ice buckets. It was empty.

I filled it in the bathroom, doused it on the burning couch cushion, noticing to my surprise it had been turned over, bottom-side up.

After I'd opened the windows and was able to draw a decent breath I tried to wake up the white-haired hotshot by pulling him off the sofa. He slid to the floor in a sitting position, opened his eyes and stared blearily at me. Either he was a hard sleeper or too drunk to appreciate what had happened. He simply lounged there in a stupor while I hoisted the sofa cushion, carried it into the bathroom, dumped it into the shower.

As I did, I noticed the top of the cushion was already soaking, with a big char spot burned deeply into it.

Then I found the bottom of the Lawson was burning, too. I doused that, pulled the sofa away from the wall. The carpet underneath was also smouldering, with a half-square foot already in black, feathery ash.

By the time I put *that* out, the white-haired lad had rolled over on his face, was fast asleep again. On his undershirt, over his left shoulder blade, was a brown and black spot where heat had singed the cotton cloth. He'd fallen asleep smoking, had dropped his lighted cigarette on the cushion beside him, rolled over and slept until the heat of the smouldering stuffing had roused him.

Then he'd gotten up, slopped some of the melted ice-cube water on it, turned the mattress over and gone back to sleep . . . with the fire still burning!

The topper to that one was that when I finally did get the man awake, to make sure he hadn't inhaled enough of those poisonous fumes to hurt him, he cussed me out six ways to the ace.

However, things of that kind were unintentional, if criminally careless. The boy hotels hate most is the man who's criminally careful—about the damage he does. The man or woman who burns or slashes with malice aforethought.

I've been told, by doctors who specialize in mental disorders, that persons of this sort are always potentially dangerous in a physical sense, as well. As I understand it, they aren't legally insane; they merely take out some fancied grudge in viciously doing all the harm they can to property. But the psycho sharps contend they may react violently and unpredictably when cornered or accused.

This may be true. I had to handle one case, a Charles Y——, a draughtsman in the office of a firm of prominent architects. He wasn't technically a guest of the New York hotel where I was employed at the time, but he was for some time a regular at lunch in the dining room. Usually he ate alone.

He was quickly marked as an undesirable patron by Lucien, the headwaiter in our main dining room. Y—— always argued with his waiter, often sent food back to the kitchen as not being prepared to suit him. He frequently disputed the *addition,* always left an insufficient tip. But these were not the things which incensed Lucien.

Y—— would doodle on the tablecloth, using his fountain pen. He never ate butter, but apparently feeling that he was entitled to do whatever he liked with it since he was paying for it anyway, he would sprinkle pepper on the pat and mash it around with his fork—a senseless bit of bad taste. He would break open rolls and not touch them. The blowoff, however, came about as a result of the sugar.

In our dining room sugar was served at the tables in heavy silver bowls with removable lids. One noon when he noticed Y—— grinding out his cigarette in the sugar bowl, Lucien went pale. He rushed across to Y——'s table, the draughtsman was alone, and ordered the guest out of the dining room. Y—— refused to go until he was good and ready. Lucien, enraged beyond control, began to drag the man out of his chair.

I happened to be in the lobby; I got into it in time to prevent a knockdown and drag-out. Y—— was ejected, and went with no more protest than a threat to come back and get even. If he ever did I never heard about it.

In my experience, the loudmouth ones who bluster the most aren't as dangerous as the quiet ones who never let you know how vicious their intentions may be.

One evening in midsummer, about six years ago, I was having a bean-feast with the Assistant Banquet Manager. I like good cheese; sometimes after one of the swanky shindigs there'd be some Stilton in port or good imported Camembert left over; I'd be invited to a snack up in my friend's office. Usually there'd be something pretty special to wash the cheese and raw apple down with, too. But this time, before we really got down to work, the alarm hit in.

There was a slasher in the house.

A slasher is some warped individual who cuts, rips and mutilates upholstery, leather, curtains and sometimes employees' uniforms. The tool usually employed is a safety razor blade, though I have met up with one slasher who used a broken piece of bottle.

The damage this slasher had done was almost incredible; new reports kept coming in every ten minutes all evening long.

The first news had come from the cocktail lounge. From two adjoining red-leather banquettes triangular pieces about an inch long had been sliced out of the leather by three overlapping slashes. This fellow was making sure the damage couldn't be fixed by any ordinary repair methods.

In the lobby he'd cut more of those triangular pieces out of sofas, out of the long eighteen-foot draperies, out of two high-backed settees done in tapestry. On the mez . . . only a hundred feet or so from my office . . . he'd mutilated the leather seat of a Spanish chair which was a sort of showpiece.

By midnight a rough estimate of the damage would have been five thousand dollars at the least. The Front Office was in a real sweat.

There was a possibility, of course, that by the time most of the damage had been discovered, the slasher had already left the hotel, might not return. In which case, trying to find him would be an almost impossible job.

I had to proceed on the assumption he was still around. My first thought was of some disgruntled employee or ex-employee. We'd once had an elevator operator who'd found out he was to be fired and had tried to get even by setting off a stink bomb he'd bought at a Broadway novelty store: he'd dropped it in the bottom of the elevator shaft!

But a hectic checking with every employee who'd been in or around the lobby from six o'clock on gave me no lead in that direction at all. Then I tried to dope out if it could be some guest who'd imagined he'd had a grievance and had tried to take it out on the furnishings.

I asked every bellman, the desk clerks, the assistant managers, the elevator operators, the room-service waiters. None of them could give me any help except to turn in a few more choice examples of the mutilator's handiwork.

There were still seventy-five or a hundred people moving in and around the lobby. I stood by the main stairway to the street, racking my brains to figure out which of them might be the person we had to find before he slashed another five thousand dollars' worth of furniture to ribbons.

Finally I tried the old mule trick. You remember, the lost mule and the dumb farm boy who found him, when nobody else could, by "figurin' where I'd go if I was a mule an' I went thar an' he had"? Where, I asked myself, would I go if I was sore at the world or at somebody in particular and wanted to nurse my grudge alone?

To the bar! Sure. So I "went thar," asked the bartenders. One of them finally remembered "a little guy, mean-looking little guy, kept mumbling to himself about a check."

That wasn't much, but it was a starter. I went to hunt up the Credit Manager. He'd gone to bed.

There were calls for me from the Assistant Managers, from the Resident Manager's office. More damage was being reported by bellmen every half-hour. I stuck with the old mule system.

When I got the Credit Manager out of bed and asked him if he'd refused to cash a check for some guest that evening, he said he had; he'd turned down half a dozen as he did every day in the week.

I wanted to know if one of them had been "a little fellow, mean-looking little fellow?" That, the Credit Manager admitted, would have fitted one of the individuals he'd turned down. Fellow'd wanted a couple hundred dollars, had been told he'd have to wait until morning when the Credit Office could get in touch with his bank by phone.

But he couldn't remember the bird's name! He'd recall it if he heard it again . . . Cazza Kazan? Something foreign-sounding.

I got the Information Clerk on the phone, had him read off every foreign-sounding name on the Rack. At *Edouard Lazani,* we hit it.

I checked the registration. Mr. Lazani had signed in from Lynn, Massachusetts. Had been in the hotel two days. Was in Room 1279. N.P.R. was marked on his card; there was No Previous Record of Mr. Lazani in the Guest History files.

He was still in the hotel.

For the next twenty minutes I did some fast checking. One of the elevator operators remembered taking the man to his room around quarter past eleven. Bellmen recalled him as being around the lobby for quite a while during the evening, had thought him moody, probably lonely. Hadn't seen him speak to anyone.

A porter thought he'd run into the fellow on the mezzanine. The girl on the newsstand could "almost swear" the little man had spent several minutes standing over by the long gold brocaded draperies which had been ruined.

I sent a patrol up to watch the corridor outside 1279.

We held a council in the Resident Manager's suite, two of the Assistant Managers, the Credit Manager, the R.M. and I. By then our credit man had burnished up his memory sufficiently to recall that Lazani had seemed extremely incensed at the refusal to advance him cash on his check; his eyes had had "a sort of wild look in them," etc.

Still, we couldn't rap on a guest's door and accuse him offhand. I suggested I go up, get in the man's room on some pretext, look around. If the fellow was off his rocker to the extent of inflicting six or seven thousand dollars worth of damage to hotel property *downstairs,* he might possibly have used his razor on chairs or bedding in his room upstairs. They agreed it was worth a try.

With one of my own staff and two Assistant Managers waiting quietly behind me, I knocked on the 1279 door.

A thin, sullen voice asked what I wanted.

"Fire Inspection," I called. "Have to check the pressure in your bathroom pipes, sir."

"Wait a minute."

It was more than a minute. During that time my patrol was down on his hands and knees peeking through the narrow slit between the sill and the bottom of the door. He whispered: "He's scurrying around in his bare feet . . . all over the place . . . can't see what he's up to."

Lazani opened up. I barged right in with a, "Sorry to disturb you, sir." One look at the man told me he was scared stiff. One look at the room told me why.

He was in his pajamas. His clothes were draped over two chairs and his shirt was lying on the carpet right out in the middle of the room. He sat on the edge of the bed with a blanket pulled over his lap, watching me as if he thought I was going to slug him.

What I did was pick up the shirt as if to do him a favor. Beneath the shirt was a triangle of brown wood, showing where a piece had been carved right out of the carpet!

I called: "All right, boys. Come on in." Then I pulled the clothing off the chairs; the fabric of backs and seats had been hacked out as if someone had taken a hatchet to them.

He never attempted to deny causing the damage. Nor would he, when we finally had him down in the Security Office, explain why the refusal to cash his check had so incensed him.

They took him to the psychiatric ward at Bellevue Hospital for sanity tests.

Next day we got the story. He was sane enough to know right from wrong. All he'd admit was that he was a moderately rich man, was prepared to pay for the damage he'd done. A phone call to his bank backed him up on it, he was worth close to a hundred thousand dollars.

205

That particular slasher was indicted, tried, convicted, sentenced to a short term in the workhouse for the damage he'd done to the hotel. If he'd been punished for what he'd taken out of me, during that bad couple of hours, he'd be doing time yet.

XIX

The Respectful Prostitutes

SOMEBODY has defined a convention as a lot of loose spenders getting tight. To be sure, the consumption of alcoholic beverages isn't slowed down any by the gathering of the business and professional clans. But at the hotels for which I've worked, at which there'd be some regional or national get-together forty out of every fifty-two weeks, liquor was never as big a problem as sex.

Offhand I could name a score of prominent business organizations at whose annual *kaffee klatches* more girls were made than speeches, and those boys were no slouches at the after-dinner orations, either. I've had members of national trade associations admit to me that the principal reason they made it to the yearly talk-fest was to be able to "play around a few nights"—which they never dared to do back in their home towns.

The sort of girls who provide this stimulating entertainment for community-leaders-away-from-home are very different from the Commercial Artists. Most Convention Cuties couldn't be classed as prostitutes by any stretch of the term, though virtually all do swap intimacies for gifts or money before the evening is over.

Some will be employees of a company whose sales manager has an axe to grind with convention delegates. One may be a stenographer for a trade publication whose editor or advertising manager finds it advantageous to be "in with the boys." Or a model acquainted with the junior executive who's been assigned to see the friends of the firm "don't get lonesome while in town."

Many of them will have been "arranged for," some time in advance of the evening when they will join the festivities . . . or provide it. A few may be spur-of-the-moment inspirations; once up in the hotel suite a secretary, primed with a couple of drinks, may be induced to call up a young housewife "whose husband works nights," or "a girl I used to know in college," to get her over to the hotel.

If the Convention Cutie has been around enough to know how such things should be handled, she may be told, before she gets too far involved, that under no circumstances shall she take any money from the "friend of the firm" or the "important customer." The company, she will be given to understand, will fix all that up with her later.

All she has to do is "be a good kid." Or "see he has a good time, *you* know!" It is made clear that the "friend" or the "customer" may *spend* money on her, take her out dancing later in the evening, to one of the Harlem hot spots or possibly even to one of the "exclusive" Café Society joints. What happens after that is up to her. But there must be no crude asking for "the price of that nifty suit" or any of those gimme-girl dodges.

Though all of these Cuties know just about what to expect, once they get up in a hotel room where a bunch of the boys are whooping it up, still they're expected to pretend they *don't* know. This makes for higher blood pleasure on the part of the big customer, who likes to think it's his terrific personal charm which causes the Cutie to break down, finally, "I don't want you to think I *would,* with just *anybody! . . .* But somehow you're *different!"*

Some of the pretended shyness may be actual, due to lack of experience or fear of consequent pregnancy, etc. But whether real or put on, the reluctance must be part of the act. One girl told me, after I'd had to break up a party which was becoming too boisterous: "Why, I never even took my *hat* off." Few do take off their hats . . . or anything else . . . right away.

I always went very lightly on convention parties. This was because, in many cases, nothing more than the get-acquainted stages would take place in *our* hotel. Couples would become friendly after four or five drinks, decide there might be more exciting things to do than barber-shop *Down By The Old Mill Stream,* and depart.

If the stenographer had to explain to her folks that she'd stayed overnight with a gal-pal, or the young house-wife seemed sleepier than usual to her husband the next day, that was none of my business.

But there was another reason I wore my best kid gloves when investigating any complaint which had to do with rooms on a convention floor. If Sam Jones, in from Wichita on business, raised any objectionable rumpus I could deal with him and any female he might have sneaked up to his room. But if someone suggested I quiet the disturbance in the suite of Bill Smith, in from St. Louis as a delegate to a big convention, I had to keep in mind Mr. Smith had several hundred friends in the house. Any or all of them might resent it if the hotel dealt harshly with him.

If Smith had been tippling and if there were several Cuties in his rooms, he might feel compelled to throw his weight around, to demonstrate what a big shot he was. Many a reputable citizen would, when teed up, become violently incensed over a fancied insult to some girl he'd hardly have been able—or willing—to recognize twenty-four hours later.

There was another angle. One disgruntled delegate might—even if he had no reason whatever to object when I'd asked him to "tone it down a bit, please"—influence others in his group to select some other hotel next time the conclave was held in our city. When, as, and if such information came boomeranging back to the Convention Manager, I might have had to hunt for a new berth. I had one close call in that connection with Dr. C——.

Dr. C—— was a chemical tycoon, the brains and Board Chairman of a concern which dominated its branch of the industry. Also, he pretty well ran a regional association which held its annual paper-readings, etc. at our hotel. He was around eighty, tall, skinny, white-haired and cold-eyed, with a sarcastic manner of speech.

I don't know whether the younger men who were in Dr. C——'s suite that evening really liked the old boy or whether they were merely anxious to stay on his good side. But it was clear to me that he wanted very much to be considered one of the boys, still a regular fellow . . . even at eighty.

He had a big double suite on the fifth floor; from it the strains of

Virgin sturgeon
Need no urgin'

were drifting upward and disturbing other guests all the way up to the Eighth. After one in the morning, complaints began to come in every quarter-hour.

I made one phone call with a mild suggestion that the

boys cut the muffler in; Dr. C—— was rather caustic at his end.

Half an hour later I had to go up, rap on the door. The sounds of revelry included hilarious feminine squeals.

Dr. C—— opened the door himself. He was dignified-drunk. A twenty-year-old redhead had one arm around his neck; she was pretty far gone, too. Her shoes were off; she kept doing a kind of tango-step in her stocking feet. Her eyes had that glassy look which told me she'd pass out any minute.

There were two other Cuties; both blondes, neither feeling any pain. One lay on her back on the sofa with her stocking knees—and plenty of pink nylon—showing. The other sat on the lap of a middle-aged bird who looked like an engineer. Two younger men sat on the floor, heads propped against the sofa. They waited expectantly for the Doctor to tell me off.

He did.

I said it was a shame to interrupt such a swell party but, to make it easier on me, couldn't they lower the level of the loud-speaker a little.

He glared at me; I suppose that truculent glare had brought many a Board meeting into line. "If the walls of your damned hotel," he said acidly, "are so damned thin that our quiet little party's keeping others awake, then by God next time we hold a convention it'll be some place where they can accommodate us without any damned inconvenience to others!"

I was sure he wouldn't want to deprive anyone of the good night's rest I hoped he and his friends would enjoy.

One of the young men on the floor guffawed. "Think that's *all* we're going to enjoy?" He stroked the upraised knees.

Doctor C—— kept those cold eyes on me. "Next year

we'll find some place where no damned wart-head can bother us every fifteen minutes all evening long, understand?!"

I said I was sorry he felt that way and when he slammed the door in my face, I *was*. From what I'd heard about him down at the Main Desk I knew he had influence enough to make plenty of trouble for me at the Front Office.

Still I had my job to do. When another angry complaint came from across the hall, half an hour later, I went up to the Doctor's suite again.

This time the man who might have been an engineer opened the door. Doctor C—— wasn't in sight; neither was the redhead. The doors to both bedrooms were closed. The girl on the sofa looked as if she'd gone to sleep. The other blonde was shaking her. The two younger men were killing the last of a quart of bourbon and sniggering at each other like a couple of conspirators.

"Party's jus' breakin' up," the engineer smirked.

"Yeah," one of the sniggerers chimed in, "we're takin' th' chicks home, jussa few minutes."

I said that was fine, went back downstairs.

Ten minutes later the younger men came down, each steering a blonde who was hardly able to navigate. They piled into one cab; one of the girls gave an address.

After another five minutes the engineer walked out of a Down car, by himself.

I smiled: "No hard feelings?"

"Uh, uh." He shook his head. "An' say . . . don't worry about ol' Doc blowing his valve. He'll forget all about it, by mornin'."

I said I hoped so.

"Sure," he grinned. "Keep a li'l secret?"

I thought I could.

"Well, Doc—he went to bed—had all he could handle. We had to put his pajamas on for him. Went to sleep the minute he hit the pillow." He chuckled. "Then Elsie . . . she's the redheaded one . . . *she* went out like a light. Boys thought it would be a great gag to undress *her*, put her in bed with ol' Doc. So we did. Boy, when he wakes up, he'll think he's hell on wheels. 'Course it'll all be in his mind, but I bet he doesn't raise any hell with the hotel. You wait, you'll see."

And it was even so. I saw the estimable Doctor at noon the next day; he was strutting, standing still. He was congratulating our Resident Manager on handling the convention so splendidly!

That was the only time I can recall having knowingly allowed unlawful cohabitation to take place in our establishment. Only I don't guess you could call it much of a cohabiting, at that.

While most Convention Cuties are recruited from the office forces, the sales personnel or the casual acquaintances of the executives entrusted with "seeing that the boys enjoy themselves," sometimes there aren't enough of them to go around. Or possibly they might be, in the opinion of the official procurer, too tame to satisfy some of the more sophisticated customers.

Then somebody will suggest the call houses. Address books with lists of cryptic phone numbers will be consulted; at the desired time, a couple of the more experienced Ladies of the Evening will show up. Usually there'll be only two of these, partially because items of $100 per Entertainer are more difficult to camouflage on expense accounts, but more particularly since they're being hired to put on an exhibition, a *circus*.

These affairs, generally staged in a roomful of well-primed younger men, set two girls to undressing to the tune of lewd . . . and crude . . . suggestions from the onlookers. Sometimes the boys get more than they'd bargained for, it being fairly common practice for the girls to tip off their "protectors" . . . who then arrange for a plain-clothes raid.

The usual outcome of that is a shakedown, and however innocent the hotel may have been, it always gets blamed. A couple of raided circuses can downgrade a good hotel as quickly as a quarantine for smallpox.

Aside from breaking up sessions of that sort, about all a House Officer could do on a convention floor was to see that there was no rough stuff. If a Cutie was invited up to a party and came of her own free will, that was one thing.

But once in a while some youngster would be brought along by an older girl who *did* know what it was all about, while the younger one wouldn't, and might not know how to get out of it. That's when the House Officer has a chance to do something he can feel good about, afterward. I felt that way about Della.

It happened in the Boston hotel where I was assistant to the Chief. It was one of the best houses in town at that time, though its equipment was, even then, a bit old-fashioned. Only a few of the rooms on each floor had private bathrooms; the rest had washbasins but depended for other facilities on common bathrooms located near the elevators.

There was a sales convention in the hotel at the time; the bellmen had been doing a land-office business on liquor orders, were sacking their tips in pillow slips. One of them paused long enough while making a delivery to tell me that some drunk was making a disturbance outside the bathroom on Four.

I went right up. Even before I got off the clanking

service car I could see, through the open grillwork of the elevator, a gray-haired man in a candy-striped silk shirt, rattling the doorknob of the bathroom.

"C'mon, kid," he was pleading through the locked door. "C'mon outa there. I'm not gonna hurt you . . . wouldn't hurt you for anything in th' world."

As I got off the car the girl in the bathroom called: "Go away! I'm sick, I tell you! Leave me *alone!*" She sounded as if she *was* sick.

I asked the drunk what the trouble was.

He gave me a wise leer. "She's just faking. We were havin' a little fun an' she got mad, that's all."

"Maybe if you go back to your room and let me talk to her, I can get her to come out," I told him. "Why don't you let me see what I can do with her?"

He hiccoughed that if I could do anything with her I was a better man than he was; he'd been trying all night, with no luck. He weaved away, down the corridor.

After a gentle tap on the door I called: "He's gone, miss. This is the House Officer. It's all right to come out."

She opened the door and I had a surprise. She was stunningly beautiful, even with tears streaking mascara over her cheeks. But she couldn't have been a day older than seventeen, if that. And she didn't have any dress on, or any shoes.

"I can't come out," she blubbered, "I can't, looking like this!"

"Where's your dress?" I asked.

"In his room. He . . . he told me he'd give me ten dollars if I'd just take it off and . . . let him *look* at me . . ." she whimpered, "and like a fool I thought he meant it. He promised he wouldn't touch me . . . but . . ."

"How'd you happen to be in his room?"

"I came up with a friend . . . Anna . . . she said a couple of nice gentlemen wanted to show us some samples of . . . of lingerie."

"Where's Anna?"

"She . . . she went away with the other man . . . left me alone with that fellow. When he started pawing . . . oh! it was awful . . . I wouldn't go back there again for a million dollars . . . and he's got my dress . . . and shoes!" She wailed.

"You wait here," I said "I'll get your things."

The drunk was staggering back toward us. "I *tol'* you she was faking!"

I said she wasn't faking, that he was in serious trouble.

He sobered a little. "Whatcha mean, serious!"

I told him the girl was underage, had said he'd tried to attack her.

"I never touched her! Swear to God I didn't! She's lying if she says I did."

I said it looked mighty bad, that by rights I ought to call the precinct.

He did everything but go down on his knees. "Don't do that! For God's sake! You don't know what that'd mean to me!"

For a few minutes I let him sweat. He took out his wallet, held out a sheaf of bills.

It was a temptation; I could let him think he was bribing me and turn the money over to that poor frightened kid.

Then I decided that might give her the wrong idea, that she might get away with something again and get paid off, without getting hurt. So I told the old lecher to keep his money; if the girl decided to make a complaint, I said, he'd need it for a bail bond.

He looked pretty sick, then.

I took the dress and shoes back to the bathroom. "By rights I ought to take you home and tell your folks about this."

"Please, please, *please!*" she begged. "I'll never do anything like that again, if you'll just not tell my father! *Please* say you won't!"

"If I was your father," I said, "I'd give you one hell of a good whaling. Go on home. And stay away from hotel rooms."

"I hope I never see the inside of a hotel room again in my whole life," she sniffled, putting on her shoes.

That was the last I saw of her. But I expect maybe she changed her mind about hotel rooms. She probably married some decent young fellow; chances are she didn't spend her honeymoon on a cruise ship.

XX

Collans, Speaking

IF THERE'S any better place than a hotel to see the ups and downs of human nature, I don't know where it is. The House Officer, especially, sees people at their best or worst, in high spirits or down in the dumps. One person will be gay and cheerful, looking forward to meeting a friend, planning on having a hot time in the old town. Another will be coming back to his room after a tiring day, possibly depressed at knowing no one to whom he can talk, at having no place to go in the strange city.

Then, too, few people behave the same way away from home as when they're in their own back yard. Some get a lift out of new surroundings, become exhilarated at being without the usual responsibilities of friends or family. Others become more aloof, stand on their dignity because they're not at ease among strangers.

Of course, it's just these ever changing attitudes on the part of different guests which make a House Officer's job so interesting. The problems have changed some since I started in the business, but the guests have changed less than anything else. Hotels have become more efficient, more convenient, most comfortable. Possibly, just possibly, they've lost, in the process of improvement, some of the personal touches which used to make a guest feel at home when he walked up to the mail desk in the "good old days." Or were they so good, when it took half an hour to run a bath or get a pitcher of ice water?

Air-conditioning, television in every room, the clock in the radio by which you can set your own morning call to wake up musically . . . all wonderful. And the guests are still wonderful, too. But with all the complicated apparatus of modern hotel efficiency, the Front Office hasn't yet found a way to replace the House Officer with electric eyes. I don't expect they will.

So I can keep right on envying the boys who're holding down the job I used to like so much. It was a swell job. In my opinion, Riley never lived a better life.

D. C.

TERMS LIKE THESE ARE HOTELESE

Bathroom Bertha. Female guest who ducks into bathroom to avoid tipping bellman; male equiv., Bathroom Benny.

Comp. Nonpaying guest, usually on a due-bill taken in exchange for advertising.

Cuter. Quarter; one who habitually tips two-bits.

Deemer. One who gives dimes as gratuities.

Deuce. Table set for two.

Display. Key given guest who wishes no employees to enter his room.

Fasullo. A phony.

Fishing. Buildup for a tip.

Frisco. To case a guest's room and luggage.

Front. Bellman next on call, sometimes referred to as the "stick."

Greeter. Registration clerk.

Hoper. Prospective guest without registration, waiting for cancellation.

Hot-pillow House. Cheap hotel which rents a room several times a night.

Ledge. Bell Captain's ledger, record of errands.

Nit. A nuisance; also, sometimes a poor tipper.

No Show. Reservation which didn't claim room.

Plug. Master key to lock door against nonpaying guest.

Put-out. Ejection of guest from room.

Rack. Card file of guest roomings.

Riding Academy. Hotel not too particular about respectability.

Sheet. Daily Function Sheet, posted in elevators, etc.

Side Money. What an employee nets on tips.

Skipper. Guest who leaves without paying bill.

Sleeper. Account carried as active beyond departure date of desk.

Sleep-out. Guest who pays for occupancy but does not stay in room for night.

Sniffer. Nighttime floor patrol, on alert for smoke from beneath doors, etc.

Snooter. Headwaiter.

Stuff. Drugs, often sleeping tablets or benzedrine.

Tray. Room-service table.

Tweenies. Kitchen assistant, not a chambermaid.

Trucker. Guest with excessive baggage.

Under A Flag. Using a phony name, an alias.

Walk. Airing guest's pooch.

Watch. Room or guest on Security man's Observation list.

Wino. Guest who drinks heavily in room but not in bar.

Note: Hotel vernacular, like that developed in other trades, varies widely with locality; hence some of the terms listed above apply to certain sections of the country only.

S. S.